HIDDEN
HISTORY
of
NEW JERSEY
at WAR

HIDDEN
HISTORY
of
NEW JERSEY
at WAR

JOSEPH G. BILBY,
JAMES M. MADDEN AND
HARRY ZIEGLER

Charleston  London

THE
History
PRESS

Published by The History Press
Charleston, SC 29403
www.historypress.net

Copyright © 2014 by Joseph G. Bilby, James M. Madden and Harry Ziegler
All rights reserved

First published 2014

Manufactured in the United States

ISBN 978.1.62619.178.5

Library of Congress CIP data applied for.

This book is dedicated to the state of New Jersey's soldiers and their families and to those who supported them, and continued to do so, on the battle front and the homefront.

CONTENTS

CONTENTS

ACKNOWLEDGEMENTS

No project like this can be accomplished through the efforts of the authors alone, and we would like to acknowledge the valuable assistance of John Beekman of the Jersey City Free Public Library, Ed Civinskas, New Jersey State Police archivist Mark Falzini, Ernie Giudci, Dan Lane, Sergeant First Class (ret.) Duncan MacQueen, Robert Perricelli and Fred Carl of InfoAge Museum, Cory Newman, Robert Rudinski, New Jersey National Guard Militia Museum curator Captain Vincent Solomeno and Steve Southwick. Our thanks are due to all, as are our apologies to anyone we inadvertently missed.

INTRODUCTION

*H*idden *History of New Jersey at War* is not a comprehensive military history of the state, a much-needed work that is yet to be done. It is, however, a series of essays that deal with various little-known aspects of the state's military experience, from Henry Hudson's first contact with New Jersey's Native Americans in 1609 through the War for Independence, in which the state has been accurately characterized as the "Crossroads of the Revolution," and the War of 1812 and the Mexican War, in which New Jersey's participation has gone largely unrecorded, into the national crucible of the Civil War, the "Splendid Little War" against the Spanish in 1898, World Wars I and II, Korea, Vietnam and the Cold War. There are tales of generals and privates, soldiers and civilians, heroism and blundering, on the war front and the homefront, all capturing how the state's citizens coped with the struggles thrust upon them by the inexorable tide of history.

CHAPTER I

THE FIRST SHOT

The first verified fatal shot fired by residents of New Jersey directed against an outside enemy was from a bow, not a gun.

Before the coming of the Europeans, the Lenape, New Jersey's Native American people, were inhabitants of the larger homeland of *Lenapehoking*, a territory covering portions of several modern states, including New York, Maryland, Pennsylvania and Delaware, as well as New Jersey. The Lenape were members of the Minsi or Munsee (north) and Unami (central and south) language subgroups. As far as modern archaeologists can estimate, they and their forebears had been residents of *Lenapehoking* for up to twelve thousand years.

The original meaning of the word "Lenape," which has slight variant pronunciations in Minsi and Unami, has been variously interpreted and disputed over the years. Late Seton Hall University archaeologist Herbert Kraft, the leading expert on New Jersey's Indians, wrote that it might have several meanings, including "real person," or "men of the same nation." The Lenape were not a "nation" in the European sense of the word but an aggregation of small bands of connected families with a similar language, although Unami and Munsee speakers were not necessarily completely intelligible to each other.

The limited number of warriors available, coupled with local feuds between bands—Lenape in central New Jersey, for example, reputedly detested those living on Manhattan Island—and a decentralized political structure severely limited overall Lenape war-making capability, as raising significant military organizations and engaging in large-scale combat involving heavy casualties and widespread destruction were impossible. One early European observer noted that "it is a great fight where seven or eight is slain." Inter-band violence did occur, as evidenced by the discovery, in 1895, of a Staten Island burial in which the deceased was apparently shot by thirty-three arrows, but it was limited in scope. We have no written or traditional accounts of what these conflicts were about, but squabbles over hunting and fishing territories or personal enmity based on some sort of grudge can be assumed. Kraft, however, reported that "very few" excavated Lenape burials "show evidence of warfare or death through violence."

At the time of European contact, the chief Lenape weapon was the "self bow," which, although similar in length, contrasted unfavorably in power with the English longbow, as well as the composite or laminate bow used by other Native Americans. Hand-to-hand combat weapons included war clubs of various types. (A ball-headed club, probably Lenape, from the New Sweden colony along the Delaware River, survives in Skokloster Castle in Sweden.) Arrowheads and knives were chipped from flint at the time of first contact between natives and Europeans. Lenape tactics were simple and limited to ambushes and surprise raids on rival groups. The Lenape code required that killings in war or personal feuds be avenged, but the continual spiral of violence that this belief suggests could be, and usually was, short-circuited by negotiations and payments to relatives of the deceased. Interestingly, in these settlements, the lives of women were apparently considered more important than those of men. Lenape concepts of war and peace, as well as property ownership, would change dramatically with the arrival of Europeans in *Lenapehoking*.

The first known European to sail along the present New Jersey shore was Giovanni de Verrazzano, an Italian employed by King Francis I of France with orders to find a passage through America to the Orient. In the spring of 1524, Verrazzano reached the coast of today's North Carolina and then headed north, vainly seeking the nonexistent passage. As the Native Americans along the shore of *Lenapehoking* observed Verrazzano's ship, *La Dauphine*, glide by, it is doubtful that they remotely anticipated what was in store for them and their descendants over the next two centuries. One thing that can be said for sure, however, is that they were not afraid of the Europeans. When *La Dauphine* rounded Sandy Hook into Raritan Bay, which Verrazzano called *Santa Margarita*, large numbers of Lenape rushed down to the shore with great excitement, launching canoes to get a closer look at the white men. Prevailing winds prevented a landing, however, postponing a face-to-face meeting between Lenape and Europeans. There is no existing evidence of any closer encounters between the two cultures for the rest of the sixteenth century, although one or more are certainly possible, even probable, considering that a number of European fishermen and explorers sailed into American waters over those years.

The next verifiable contact between the Lenape and Europeans in what is now New Jersey occurred when Henry Hudson, an Englishman exploring on behalf of the Dutch, entered Raritan Bay in 1609. The Dutch had created an independent state from an obscure province of Spain that then became the Netherlands, a rising maritime power in the seventeenth-century world. Hudson, yet another explorer seeking the elusive "Northwest Passage" through North America to the Orient, was the first European to make documented physical contact with the Lenape of present-day New Jersey. As in 1524, the Indians demonstrated no fear of their visitors, but on this occasion, what began as a series of seemingly innocuous trading opportunities ended badly. The lack of trust, cultural insensitivity, bullying and outright theft that Hudson's men displayed during a number of forays into Raritan and New York Bays resulted in several deadly incidents, including one in which a sailor was killed when hit in the throat by a flint-tipped arrow and another in which eight or ten Lenape were blown out of the water and several canoes sunk by small arms and artillery fire from Hudson's ship, the *Half Moon*. The unfortunate European fatality, one John Colman, was reportedly buried on Sandy Hook, the first recorded European combat casualty suffered in today's New Jersey. Likewise, the unnamed

A Lenape village at the time of Henry Hudson's voyage, as portrayed in a 1930 diorama at the Public Museum of Staten Island. *From Kull,* New Jersey History.

Francis Davis Millet's *Repulse of the Dutch*, depicting the 1609 death of John Colman, in the Hudson County Courthouse. *Jersey City Free Public Library.*

Lenape sprayed with fire from Hudson's ship were the first New Jerseyans to become combat casualties. Hudson had more luck trading farther up the river that today bears his name, where he swapped some metal hatchets and hoes, whiskey and wine for beaver pelts, corn and tobacco.

A late nineteenth-century impression of the Lenape first shot and death of Colman, a mural by Francis Davis Millet entitled *Repulse of the Dutch*, endures in the Hudson County Courthouse in Jersey City to this day, although the victim in this case was, as was Hudson, English-born. Millet, a Massachusetts native, Civil War veteran, Harvard graduate, international celebrity artist, war correspondent and possible lover of travel writer Charles Warren Stoddard, was considered by many the best muralist of his day. Born in 1848, he died in the sinking of the *Titanic* on April 15, 1912.

The only surviving account of Hudson's voyage and Colman's death is in a journal kept by Robert Juet, a member of Hudson's crew. What follows is an account of the first shot from Robert Juet's journal of the Hudson voyage:

> *The sixth* [of September 1609], *in the morning, was faire weather, and our Master sent John Colman, with foure other men in our Boate, over to the North-side to sound the other River, being foure leagues from us. They found by the way shoald* [shallow] *water, two fathoms; but at the North of the River eighteen, and twentie fathoms, and very good riding for Ships; and a narrow River to the Westward, betweene two Ilands. The Lands, they told us, were as pleasant with Grasse and Flowers and goodly Trees as ever they had seene, and very sweet smells came from them. So they went in two leagues and saw an open Sea, and returned; and as they came backe, they were set upon by two Canoes, the one having twelve, the other fourteene men. The night came on, and it began to rayne, so*

Top: A bust statue of Henry Hudson, in memory of his exploratory voyage, stands in Jersey City's Riverside Park. *James M. Madden.*

Right: Henry Hudson's ship the *Half Moon* as portrayed in a nineteenth-century account of his voyage. *James M. Madden.*

that their Match went out; and they had one man slaine in the fight, which was an English-man, named John Colman, with an Arrow shot into his throat, and two more hurt. It grew so darke that they could not find the ship that night, but labored to and fro on their Oares. They had so great a streame, that their grapnell would not hold them.

For further reading, see Kraft, Lenape-Delaware Indian Heritage; *Dowd,* The Indians of New Jersey; *Boyd,* Atlantic Highlands; *Moss,* Monmouth: Our Indian Heritage; *and Lender,* One State in Arms.

Chapter 2

KIEFT'S WAR

Henry Hudson failed to discover a northwest passage, but his success in trading trinkets and liquor for valuable furs inspired Dutch merchants to follow in his wake. They established a trading post called Fort Orange at today's Albany and may also have built another temporary post on the site of modern Jersey City in 1614.

Control over the growing colony of New Netherland was granted to the Dutch West India Company, and in 1624, the company founded several settlements, including New Amsterdam on Manhattan Island, to provide support and supplies to the trading posts. Many early settlers were not "Dutch" as the term is understood today and included Walloons from what is now Belgium and French Huguenots and other groups fleeing religious wars and persecution in Europe. New Netherland became an extremely diverse place, and by one account, there were eighteen different languages in use in the capital, New Amsterdam, in 1643.

In an attempt to encourage more settlements, the company granted "patroonships," or large plots of land, along the North (Hudson) River to wealthy merchants, who were, in turn, obligated to establish farming communities on the grants. Michiel Reyniersz Pauw received such a grant across the river from New Amsterdam in 1630. His land, called Pavonia after him, stretched from modern Staten Island to Hoboken and was the first permanent European settlement in today's New Jersey.

Few colonists moved to Pauw's Pavonia. It reverted to West India Company control, and the company leased land to settlers who combined farming with fur trading. Pavonia grew slowly, as tension increased between settlers and natives. European domestic animals wandered through Indian fields, rooting up maize and bean crops. Lenape dogs harassed the trespassing pigs and cattle in turn, and trade cheating by the Dutch and petty theft by the Indians escalated. War was perhaps inevitable, but New Netherland director general

Lenape man and woman in the seventeenth century, as portrayed in a 1930 diorama at the American Museum of Natural History. *From Kull,* History of New Jersey.

Willem Kieft dramatically accelerated the downward spiral in relations following his arrival at New Amsterdam in 1637.

Early on, Kieft ordered an attack on a band of Raritan Lenape for allegedly stealing pigs on Staten Island and then levied an arbitrary tax on local Native Americans and threatened to attack them if it was not paid. He was apparently trying to provoke a conflict he had no doubt he would win. Over the winter of 1642–43, a band of Wiechquaeskeck Lenape, driven south by marauding Mohawk, fled to New Amsterdam and then crossed the North River to the vicinity of Pavonia, where they sought refuge with the local Hackensack band.

On February 23, 1643, Kieft ordered his soldiers to conduct a surprise night attack on the refugees and Hackensacks. David Pieterz de Vries, a Dutchman who opposed Kieft, recalled, "I heard a great shrieking...and I looked over to Pavonia. Saw nothing but firing, and heard the shrieks of the savages murdered in their sleep." Kieft's troops indiscriminately killed men, women and children. Some of the latter, according to De Vries, were "hacked to pieces in the presence of the parents, and the pieces thrown into the fire and in the water." De Vries wrote that some soldiers brought human heads back across the river as trophies. Another colonist described the events as "a disgrace to our nation."

Kieft's troops, known as "sea soldiers" due to their overseas assignment to the colonies, were one-year contract employees of the West India Company. The majority of them were apparently Germans who drifted into the Netherlands seeking work, although some were English, French or Scandinavian. They were described as "men picked up with no special regard for character, experience or ability" and commanded by "commercial and military adventurers." On arrival in Amsterdam, these migrants were given food and shelter by innkeepers known as *zielverkopers*, or "sellers of souls," who, when the West India Company put out a call for soldiers, produced them. In 1644, a sea soldier enlisted for thirteen guilders a month and an *adelborst*, or "cadet," a junior noncommissioned officer, at fifteen guilders a month. The sea soldiers received a two-month advance on their salaries, payable to the *zielverkoper* for room and board.

Company soldiers were equipped with firearms and edged weapons and perhaps minimal armor but no uniforms. Officers were authorized to wear orange sashes to denote their rank, although these insignias were only worn on special occasions. The training these men received was minimal, and the attention they paid to their military duties was limited as well. The New Amsterdam garrison was between forty and fifty men strong, and by

1644, the town fort's dimensions were 250 by 300 feet, enclosing a barracks and guardhouse. Smaller garrisons were established at forts throughout the colony, including trading posts along the South (Delaware) River. At its height in 1664, the total military garrison of Dutch New Netherland numbered between 250 and 300 men, 180 of them in New Amsterdam. Director Kieft's maximum available force of full-time soldiers two decades earlier was significantly smaller.

Kieft's sea soldiers carried muskets using the matchlock ignition system, in which the gun was fired by squeezing a bar or trigger that lowered a length of glowing potassium nitrate–soaked "match cord" into a pan of priming powder to ignite the main charge. Matchlocks were the most common firearms used by the early settlers of New Netherland. The matchlock survived in Europe as an inexpensive weapon to equip large armies to the end of the seventeenth century, but the firearms of choice for individual colonists in America became the more modern wheellock- or flintlock-ignition guns. These systems, using pyrites or flint to create sparks to ignite the main charge rather than a glowing match cord, were, when properly handled, more reliable in bad weather than the matchlock and could be more rapidly and safely reloaded. By the 1650s, the New Amsterdam government requested that half its troops be armed with wheellocks and the other half with flintlocks. The same officials wanted the personal arms of New Amsterdam settlers restricted to matchlocks, apparently out of fear that they might trade or lose more modern guns through theft to the local Lenape. Ironically, there was a lively Dutch gun trade with the Iroquois through Fort Orange, however, where flintlocks were readily exchanged for furs. By 1650, many Lenape had secured flintlocks from various sources and quickly learned how to use them. One account notes, "They are exceedingly fond of guns, sparing no expense for them; and they are [so] skillful in the use of them that they surpass many Christians."

The West India Company apparently intended its inadequate little army to be supplemented by militiamen, or at least armed citizens. All settlers entering New Netherland were required to bring personally owned firearms with them, but the colony seems to have survived initially without a formal militia. Kieft's aggressive and provocative attitude toward the Lenape led to a militia law obligating all residents of New Amsterdam to provide themselves with arms and gather at a specified location when needed for an emergency. There is no indication that this legislation produced an effective military organization, nor any evidence that the law had any force across the North River in today's New Jersey.

As Native Americans sought revenge for the Pavonia massacre, what passed for a military organization in New Netherland collapsed. Neither the sea soldiers nor disorganized militia were able to handle what came to be called "Kieft's War." Although the colony's government continued to placate the powerful Mohawk, that policy had little benefit for settlers living in New Amsterdam and Pavonia. The worst came to pass. The Lenape, in keeping with their military tradition, did not form a single large army, but disparate bands, realizing that they were in an unavoidable struggle to preserve *Lenapehocking*, launched an unprecedented series of attacks on New Netherland.

Pavonia was still lightly settled—a 1639 map reveals only eight houses and no fortifications—and most of the Dutch settlers there, who appear to have been poorly armed and disorganized, were killed or fled to New Amsterdam, where they eked out an existence as impoverished refugees as escalating violence left New Netherland only a tiny toehold on the west bank of the North River. The war spread rapidly across the colony in the opening act in an off-and-on struggle that would endure for years. Word of Kieft's treacherous attack traveled rapidly along the Lenape grapevine, and Aert Theunisen, trading along the Navesink River to the south in today's Monmouth County, was killed by local Indians seeking revenge for the massacre of their brothers to the north. As many as 1,500 warriors from various bands descended on Manhattan Island, killing many settlers and driving the survivors behind the walls of New Amsterdam.

The inept Kieft turned to professional Indian fighters from outside New Netherland to save his colony. He had previously encouraged the spillover population of New England to settle in uninhabited areas claimed by the Dutch, including Long Island and parts of today's Connecticut, and decided to make use of the English as emergency paid allies. Keift contracted with Connecticut captain John Underhill, who raised a 120-man force on Long Island. The ruthless Underhill had gained command experience in the bloody Pequot War and had made massacres his trademark. Underhill and his mercenaries surrounded a Lenape village in current Westchester County, New York, set the dwellings afire and tossed those who tried to escape back into the flames. The massacre was essentially a reenactment of the 1637 Missistuk (Mystic), Connecticut butchery perpetrated on the Pequot in which the captain had been a major participant, slaughtering virtually all of its 180 inhabitants. Underhill provided the war-making expertise the Dutch lacked and turned the military situation around. Both sides agreed to an uneasy truce in August 1645, but in the wake of his disastrous policies, combined

A statue of Pieter Stuyvesant was erected in Jersey City in 1913 to commemorate the founding of Bergen, located in today's Jersey City, shown in the map behind him. *James M. Madden.*

with complaints about his dictatorial methods by prominent citizens of New Amsterdam, Kieft was recalled to the Netherlands to explain his actions. He died in a shipwreck on the way to Europe in 1647.

Kieft was replaced by the more efficient, if similarly dictatorial, Peter Stuyvesant, and settlement in what was to become New Jersey slowly began to expand again from the tiny Pavonia bridgehead into today's Hudson County following the establishment of the town of Bergen, within the boundaries of today's Jersey City. The days of both the Dutch and Lenape were both numbered, however, and New Netherland, still periodically threatened by Indian wars due to Kieft's blundering, would last only until 1664, when it fell to the English, and the settlements west of the North River became New Jersey.

For further reading, see Shorto, Island at the Center of the World; *Kraft,* Lenape-Delaware Indian Heritage; *and Aimone, "New Netherland Defends Itself."*

CHAPTER 3

MONMOUTH COURTHOUSE

M any New Jerseyans had been ambivalent about the American War for Independence in 1775 and 1776, and a significant number of Jerseymen were Loyalists to the bitter end, but British bungling and looting had pushed the majority toward the Patriot camp, or at least into cautious neutrality, by 1778.

The Franco-American alliance of February 1778 caused the British army in America to consolidate. General Sir Henry Clinton, who had replaced General Sir William Howe as British commander in America, was ordered to evacuate Philadelphia and return to New York City, and on June 18, Howe struck out across "the Jerseys" toward Sandy Hook, where he would meet ships to transport his men to Manhattan. Clinton's army was harassed along the way by the state's militia and Continental troops, and the redcoats, in response, "villainously plundered" civilians, despite Clinton's orders to the contrary. On the afternoon of June 26, the beleaguered British column reached Monmouth Courthouse, also known as Freehold, where Clinton halted to rest his troops.

General George Washington's army left its camps at Valley Forge and crossed the Delaware into New Jersey at Coryell's Ferry (today's New Hope). Washington called a council of war at Hopewell on June 24, where General Charles Lee argued that the Americans were incapable of standing up to Clinton's army and should simply badger the British, but other generals, their soldiers trained through the efforts of Baron von Steuben at Valley Forge, wanted to risk a possibly war-winning battle. Washington decided on a middle course and ordered a force of 1,400 "picked men" from different regiments under the Marquis de Lafayette to engage the British rear guard. On June 25, he added 1,000 men and two artillery pieces to Lafayette's force. Lee then complained that he should command the advance by right of seniority. Washington conceded, and on June 26, Lee arrived at Englishtown, within five miles of Monmouth Courthouse.

At 4:00 a.m. on June 28, Clinton's army began its march to Middletown. An hour earlier, Lee had ordered Colonel William Grayson to advance his 600 men toward the enemy. Lee followed Grayson with another 1,500 soldiers. Grayson crossed the bridge over Spotswood Middle Brook, pausing with two more creek-bed wetlands between him and General Charles Cornwallis's 2,000-man-strong rear guard. Washington, still far to the rear, ordered Lee to engage the British rear guard and sent him reinforcements. General Nathanael Greene had told his chief, "People expect something from us," and Washington agreed. The American commander saw Monmouth Courthouse as his best and last chance to initiate the limited fight for limited ends that he was looking for on ground favorable to his army.

On the field, Lee conferred with Colonel Grayson and New Jersey Militia general Philemon Dickinson. Disregarding Dickinson's advice that a further advance would make his men vulnerable to counterattack, Lee moved forward, with the Americans sticking to the woods for concealment and relief from the debilitating heat. Convinced the British were leaving, Lee, who thought there were only a few hundred enemy troops to his front, pressed his men to attack. Unfortunately, the terrain blocked his view of the field, and he did not realize that the rest of Cornwallis's division was a short distance beyond. As the British rear guard and Cornwallis's division began to deploy in response to the approaching Americans, Lee began to lose control of the situation and, at one point, confused some of his own men with the enemy. He issued a flurry of orders, which one officer recalled as erupting "with a rapidity and indecision calculated to ruin us." It was too little too late, for Cornwallis's men were rapidly approaching the American right flank. Around 12:30 p.m., Lee formally ordered a general retreat, although the order was hardly necessary. With six thousand British soldiers now bearing down on his fragmented command, he was no longer the hunter but the hunted.

Initially reluctant to pursue the retreating Americans very far, Clinton changed his mind. He had his best men, guards, grenadiers and light infantry, as well as half of his mounted dragoons, on the field and so felt confident he could score a significant victory. Clinton's elite infantry deployed into two battle lines and came on hard and fast. British lieutenant Hale of the Second Grenadiers recalled the cross-country pursuit of Lee as "a march may I never again experience," along "sand [roads] which scorched through our shoes with intolerable heat; the sun beating on our heads with a force scarcely to be conceived in Europe."

The British paused briefly to consolidate, and Clinton dispatched a detachment to move around the American left flank. Lee had halted as well but, desperate to find a secure place to make a stand, ordered another retreat. Local farmer and militia officer Captain Peter Wikoff told him that either Combs' Hill or Perrine Ridge east of the Tennent Meetinghouse were the best defensive positions in the area. Lee chose Perrine Ridge and ordered Wikoff to begin guiding troops to a position near the meetinghouse. As Lee retreated, the main American army was marching to reinforce him. Riding ahead of his main force, General Washington was advised that the American advance was rapidly retreating and dispatched aides to discover the reason.

Washington encountered Captain Wikoff guiding the Second New Jersey Regiment toward Perrine Ridge and then rode on to meet Lee on a hill east of today's Wemrock Road. There are stories spun by people who were not there asserting that Washington called Lee a "damned poltroon," among other things, but Private James Jordan, a soldier in the Second New Jersey Regiment who actually witnessed the encounter, gave a more prosaic account of Washington's words, recalling that he merely asked Lee, "What is this you have been about today?" Unsatisfied with Lee's response, Washington assumed overall command on the field but did not, contrary to popular myth, relieve Lee on the spot. Instead, he ordered him to organize the rear guard to delay the British until a solid defensive line could be established on Perrine Ridge. Two forward lines were deployed, one on a hill extending an American position in a woodlot southward and to the rear of that another, the "hedgerow" line, along a rail fence and piles of cut brush.

The British encountered stiff resistance at the first line, as General Anthony Wayne's men opened fire and dropped as many as forty redcoats killed and wounded before retreating. The dragoons and grenadiers pursued the Americans toward the hedgerow line, where they ran into another blizzard of American musket balls and artillery canister shot, which one British officer described as "the heaviest fire I have yet felt," but they once again drove the Americans back. The retreat was a disciplined fighting withdrawal across the brook, with British grenadiers in cautious pursuit. American artillery on Perrine Ridge then blasted the advancing enemy with grapeshot and canister, killing Lieutenant Colonel Henry Monckton of

A dramatized version of Washington and Lee's encounter at Monmouth Courthouse. Despite legend to the contrary, Washington was calm and controlled as he assessed the situation. *Wickimedia Commons.*

the Grenadiers, whose men were unable to retrieve his body as they hastily retreated. The Americans would withdraw no more.

The Perrine Ridge line proved invulnerable. A swamp protected the American left, and the woods behind the ridge provided a safe and shady haven for reserves. Nathanael Greene, who had been ordered to prevent a British flanking attack on the right, also made a personal reconnaissance to and beyond Combs' Hill, which overlooked the battlefield. As the line stabilized, Lee apparently tried to resume his conversation with Washington, but the still unhappy commander was too busy organizing the defense to listen to him. General Lee's command time at the Battle of Monmouth—and in the war—was over.

After a British attempt to outflank Washington on the left failed, Clinton deployed his artillery to engage the American batteries on the ridge in a two-hour duel, one of the longest of the war. The range was extreme. No guns were dismounted and casualties were limited, but the cannonade supplied a future American heroine, Molly Pitcher. Molly, whose real name was apparently Mary Ludwig Hays, was described by Private Joseph Plumb Martin as "a woman whose husband belonged to the artillery" and who

Molly Pitcher (Mary Ludwig Hayes) as portrayed in a nineteenth-century painting. While she was present at the battle and probably helped serve her husband's gun, the British infantry did not get anywhere close to her position. *Monmouth Battlefield State Park.*

helped serve a gun alongside her spouse on Perrine Ridge behind and north of Martin's position. American cannons were subsequently emplaced on Combs' Hill, outflanking the British gun line, although the range was too great for them to have much effect.

Clinton, realizing that victory was not likely and that he was running short of artillery ammunition, ordered a withdrawal to consolidate his forces closer to Monmouth Courthouse. As the British began to fall back, leaving a number of dead, dehydrated and seriously wounded men behind, Washington launched several limited attacks, including an assault on the Scottish Forty-second Foot in the Sutphin Farm orchard by a battalion of New England "picked men." The Highlanders retreated, and the Americans pursued them for a short distance. Washington attacked on the right as well, ordering General Wayne to pursue withdrawing grenadiers. Wayne's advance was shattered by a counterattack that drove him back to the hedgerow and into the fields of the Tennent Parsonage farm beyond, after which the British resumed their withdrawal, with the Americans carefully advancing again in their wake. By 6:00 p.m., Washington officially ended

The Battle of Monmouth Courthouse monument was erected in the 1880s, more than one hundred years after the battle. *Joseph G. Bilby.*

the pursuit, ordering his men to sleep on the battlefield and be prepared to renew the fight in the morning. Washington himself dozed under the stars, Lafayette alongside him, near the Sutphin farmhouse.

The fight would not be renewed. While the Americans slept, Clinton moved out of Monmouth Courthouse. The British march up the Middletown road was conducted in a thoroughly professional manner and with so little noise that Washington apparently did not realize the enemy was gone until morning, although some have suggested that the American commander, usually well informed by his militia scouts, simply decided that since he had fulfilled his immediate ends that day, it was time to let the bruised British go. Clinton arrived at Sandy Hook on June 30, where his men boarded ships for Manhattan in an efficient four-day evacuation operation.

On July 1, the American army began to march away from Monmouth Courthouse. While the army marched, it court-martialed General Lee, who had imperiously demanded a trial for perceived insults he was subjected to by his commander on the field at Monmouth. Lee lost his case, and his military career came to an end.

The exact human toll of the fighting at Monmouth Courthouse is difficult to determine. Casualty reports were inconsistent and often framed to meet the propaganda goals of either side. Estimates range as high as 1,134 British and 500 Americans killed, wounded and missing in the battle itself, although the actual total is probably in the range of a third to half of that. The dead were buried, with few exceptions, in unmarked mass graves on the battlefield, where they sleep to this day.

Monmouth Courthouse was the biggest battle ever fought within the boundaries of New Jersey. It was also the last major battle of the conflict in

The new visitor center at Monmouth Battlefield State Park. *Joseph G. Bilby.*

The interior of the new visitor center at Monmouth Battlefield State Park. #17A: alternate view of #17 *Joseph G. Bilby.*

the North, although the June 1780 fight at Springfield, New Jersey, where Continentals and militia resisted a British incursion from Staten Island, was a fairly substantial action, and the state, accurately dubbed the "Crossroads of the Revolution," was plagued with guerrilla raiding until the actual conclusion of hostilities.

The Monmouth campaign established that the Continental army had become a professional military organization and provided an opportunity to perfect the army's cooperative tactics with the local militia that had originated in 1777. That military, working with effective local political organization, spelled doom to British hopes for returning New Jersey, a state that had seemed a significant source of sympathizers less than two years before, to the loyal fold. There was no going back. The performance of the American army at the battle of Monmouth Courthouse assured that America would eventually win its independence.

For further reading, see Bilby and Jenkins, Monmouth Court House.

CHAPTER 4

PAULUS HOOK AND CAMP JERSEY CITY

NEW JERSEY'S WAR OF 1812 COMMAND CENTER

The War of 1812 is sometimes characterized as America's "Second War for Independence." When the United States declared war on Great Britain on June 18, 1812, there were a number of unresolved issues between the two countries, including trade restrictions, the forcible impressing of American sailors into the Royal Navy and British assistance to Indian tribes resisting American expansion to the west, as well as other real or perceived insults to the honor of the new nation. Some Americans had other motives for a resumption of hostilities, however, as they wished to invade and annex Canada while the British were preoccupied with their long war against Napoleon.

When the military history of New Jersey is considered, the War of 1812 is usually overlooked, as the state's role in the conflict could be considered minimal. The war was not popular among many New Jerseyans, including Quaker pacifists and others who viewed it as costly and unnecessary as well as bad for business. War with Great Britain was supported by the state's Jeffersonian Republicans, and their sympathetic news outlets, including Elizabeth's *New Jersey Journal*, hailed the new conflict with "our ancient and inveterate foe." In contrast, a number of New Jersey Federalist legislators decried the war as "inexpedient, ill-timed, and most dangerously impolitick," as well as "unjust," and called for a negotiated settlement as soon as possible.

Despite the state's ambivalence, a number of New Jerseyans joined the regular army, particularly the Fifteenth United States Infantry Regiment, which fought in Canada under the command of New Jersey native Zebulon

Pike. New Jersey governor and former Revolutionary War officer Joseph Bloomfield was appointed a general, and American naval heroes William Bainbridge and James Lawrence were both born in the state. New Jersey's largest military contribution to the war effort, however, involved supplying militiamen for brief terms of service to garrison coastal forts guarding the approaches to New York City and Philadelphia. Those militiamen would all pass through the state's major military rendezvous and supply point at Paulus Hook at one time or another.

American revolutionaries built a fort at Paulus Hook in 1776, but it fell to the British when General George Washington's army evacuated New York and retreated across New Jersey later that year. The fort was fairly simple, consisting of earthworks enclosing several barracks and a parade ground. At the time, Paulus Hook was an elevated peninsula surrounded by swamps and water with a commanding view of the Hudson River and New York Bay. During high tide and heavy storms, the end of the hook, where the fort was located, became a temporary island. The peninsula, also known as Powles Hook, was then part of Bergen County and remained so until the creation of Hudson County in 1840. It is now within the boundaries of Jersey City. Whoever sited the fort chose wisely, as it was the only area in the vicinity not flooded during Hurricane Sandy in 2013.

Paulus Hook is probably best known for a daring attack launched in 1779, when the fort was a British outpost, by Major "Light Horse" Henry Lee, a 1773 Princeton graduate and father of Civil War Confederate leader Robert E. Lee. Lee quietly infiltrated a force of about three hundred picked men through the surrounding swamps and then launched a surprise strike, capturing 158 British soldiers and physically damaging the fort before withdrawing to Hackensack as daylight approached and British forces across the Hudson River began to react. The Continental Congress subsequently awarded a medal to Major Lee and $15,000 to be distributed among the soldiers engaged in the successful attack, and an obelisk-style commemorative monument to Lee's achievement was later dedicated on the site. Although moved several times over the years, the monument still stands. Despite Lee's raid, the Paulus Hook fort remained in British hands until the evacuation of New York City in 1783.

After the war, Alexander Hamilton, the first United States treasury secretary, saw economic opportunity in Paulus Hook due to its proximity to Manhattan. Hamilton and other New York businessmen formed a corporation that purchased much of the peninsula property in 1804 (the fort itself was acquired by the federal government) and developed a plan to reclaim the swampland. Although it would take many years to completely fulfill, this project was the beginning of modern Jersey City. The hook soon became a transportation hub as merchants settled in the area and built docks. As the years went by, a raised road was constructed through the swamps to handle growing coach and wagon traffic from Newark and Elizabeth as well as Philadelphia and even Baltimore on the way to New York, although heavy rain would occasionally submerge the narrow corridor across the Harsimus marshes, creating a hazardous quagmire.

Steamboat developer Robert Fulton noted the advantageous location of Paulus Hook for commerce and started a ferry service between there and New York City. Fulton's steamboat *Jersey* took about fifteen minutes for the crossing. On July 4, 1812, shortly after the beginning of the war, Fulton's boat took part in a historic first, the transport of troops across water by steam-powered craft, as his "most excellent machine" consisting of two hulls, connected by a single platform, ferried a battery of United States regular army "flying artillery" to Manhattan. It took four trips for the *Jersey* to get four guns, caissons, limbers, twenty-seven horses and forty men across the Hudson River. The ferry would continue to serve as an important troop and supply transportation service throughout the war.

The old Paulus Hook fort was formally occupied by New Jersey militiamen called to service by Governor Bloomfield on June 20, 1812. Bloomfield's mobilization order specified that the fort would serve as a site to impart "military instruction and discipline" to the often lackadaisical militia. The initial force, eleven companies totaling three hundred men under Major Isaac Andruss, was housed in the old Revolutionary War–era barracks. New Jersey quartermaster general Jonathan Rhea had one thousand "stands of arms" transferred from a federal government agent in New York City to Jersey City in order to equip militiamen who could not supply their own weapons. On August 17, 1812, Major Andruss's detachment, militiamen from Hunterdon, Middlesex, Sussex, Monmouth and Essex Counties, moved to Port Richmond on Staten Island and remained on duty there through September 25. Over the next few years, Paulus Hook, due to its strategic location, expanded to become a major training and supply hub for the New Jersey militia.

During the course of the war, New Jersey militiamen were called out for short duty stints, averaging ninety days. They initially reported to Paulus Hook, where they were equipped and organized into units and then assigned to posts from New York City, Harlem and Staten Island to "the Highlands of Navesink" and Sandy Hook, the gateway to New York Harbor. A fort was built on Sandy Hook by the lighthouse and manned by federal volunteers known as "Sea Fencibles," who were backed up by Jersey militiamen. The militiamen were paid by the state and were not considered to be in federal service, and at times, New Jersey protested the deployment of its troops to New York posts, arguing that they were intended for state service only. Other militiamen, as well as longer service volunteer "state troops," were stationed along the coast as far south as Cape May and along the Delaware at Billingsport. In all, the New Jersey militia produced 4,681 men for service during the war. Of these, one source reports that 818 were volunteers, and 3,863 were either draftees or substitutes hired by draftees to take their places. In southern Monmouth County, potential militia draftees reportedly joined together in seven-man "clubs" to pool funds to pay $50 to a substitute if one of them was conscripted. According to one family history, Daniel Drew, an underage farm boy from New York, made his way to Paulus Hook in 1814, where he became a New Jersey soldier and pocketed a $100 substitute fee for his trouble.

On August 31, 1814, in reaction to fears of a British invasion of the New York region following the burning of Washington, D.C., New Jersey militia brigadier general William Colfax was ordered to "immediately repair to Paulus Hook and take command of the whole and give necessary orders for drawing out the remainder of the brigade assigned him, inspect the county militia companies, form them into regiments and give orders." All military equipment stored at Newark was moved to Paulus Hook, which was then occupied by 1,200 men under the command of Colonel John Frelinghuysen. Colfax formed a brigade and moved it to Sandy Hook and then established an elaborate "telegraph" signaling system involving cannon fire and the lowering or hoisting of large black and white balls on masts sited atop the Highlands to convey coded "information of the movements of the enemy… to Signal Hill on Staten Island and thence to Governor's Island or Brooklyn Navy Yard in fifteen minutes."

In the event, there was no British invasion, and aside from a July 1813 American subterfuge of hiding an armed party of sailors below decks on a local fishing boat, the *Yankee*, to capture the British schooner *Eagle* off Sandy Hook, a few foraging sorties ashore from British blockading ships provided the only New Jersey action during the war. The Treaty of Ghent officially ended hostilities on December 24, 1814, although the United States Senate did not ratify the treaty until February 15, 1815.

Although the war had caused economic stress in New Jersey with the interruption of the coastal trade, privately owned turnpike companies chartered by the legislature had proved extremely profitable to their owners. The turnpikes, New Jersey's first toll roads, provided the land transportation infrastructure of the state and were used to transport massive amounts of supplies north to the armies operating in northern New York and Canada. Philadelphia, for example, was a major uniform manufacturing center, and due to the British blockade, its manufactured goods had to cross New Jersey by road to get to New York. Unfortunately, the heavy traffic, estimated at "4,000 wagons and 20,000 horses…rumbling back and forth across the state…demolished the roads," inspiring postwar solutions that further advanced New Jersey's economy while at the same time empowering a new industrial oligarchy and complicating its politics.

As military activity increased at Paulus Hook during the course of the War of 1812, the need to house troops and store equipment in the area grew. Bergen Hill, a high and dry area overlooking Paulus Hook along the road leading from the fort to Newark was chosen as a site for what would be called "Camp Jersey City." The location was near an area that had served as a campground during the Revolutionary War and had a commanding view of not only Paulus Hook and lower Jersey City but also the entirety of New York Harbor. It was also an eminently defensible position, with only one approach from the east, via the swamp road.

A federal arsenal and gunpowder magazine were built adjacent to the camp. The arsenal remained in use as late as the Civil War, when it became a rendezvous point for New Jersey militiamen who assembled there before moving to Trenton in 1861. It subsequently saw use as a training camp for the Fifty-fourth New York Volunteer Infantry and served briefly as a military hospital until it was converted into a military supply storage warehouse.

The "Old Arsenal," as it became known locally, survived until 1877, when the deteriorating building was razed. When word spread that the arsenal was about to be demolished, relic hunters, tourists and local history buffs swarmed over the area looking for souvenirs. Before workmen began the actual destruction, an enterprising photographer appeared and had them pose in front of the building, saving its image for posterity as a postcard.

By the early twentieth century, Paulus Hook was remembered only for its Revolutionary War association, and Camp Jersey City was largely forgotten. Today, the site of the camp is occupied by William L. Dickinson Public High School. When viewing the hill on which the school stands from the New Jersey Turnpike Extension approaching the Holland Tunnel or driving up the old road that once connected Paulus Hook and Camp Jersey City (today's Newark Avenue), one can, with a little imagination, envision the

Above: The "Old Arsenal" was used to store supplies and equipment for militia units who would organize there for duty at points along the coast. *James M. Madden.*

Left: A plaque installed at Dickinson High School in 1916 commemorates the service of New Jerseyans in the war of 1812. *Jersey City Free Public Library.*

earthworks and ramparts where the garrison once stood ready to repel a possible British attack.

New Jersey's War of 1812 soldiers and sailors were largely forgotten in the century following the war. In May 1916, however, the New Jersey State Society of Daughters of the War of 1812, to the accompaniment of speakers, including Jersey City–born governor James F. Fielder, and the school band, installed a bronze memorial plaque at Dickinson High School commemorating the men who served there. The plaque, which portrays a soldier, a sailor and the camp, complete with tents, a flagpole and the arsenal, symbols of an era when Paulus Hook and Camp Jersey City played a vital role in New Jersey's defense, endures.

CHAPTER 5

THE JERSEY BOYS
TAKE CALIFORNIA

No, not the Four Seasons.

In 1845, the United States annexed Texas—a self-proclaimed independent country run by Americans following its successful rebellion against the Mexican government in 1836—as a state, despite protests and threats of war by Mexico. President James K. Polk's "Manifest Destiny" policy of westward expansion, which led to the annexation, was strongly supported in the South as an opportunity to expand the territory available to a slave-labor-based economy. An April 1846 border incident in which Mexicans attacked a small American force moving into a disputed area led to a declaration of war on Mexico by the United States Congress on May 13. The subsequent conflict, an unqualified success by American standards, both tactically and strategically, resulted in a huge geographic expansion of the country.

The war was opposed by many, including both New Jersey senators and most of the state's congressmen. New Jersey senator Jacob W. Miller characterized the conflict as a land grabbing "outrage," and the state's other senator, William L. Dayton, expressed concern that it would lead to a civil war in the United States over the expansion of slavery. Despite that, in 1847, President Polk was well received on a visit to New Jersey, and the state legislature voiced support for the troops and General Zachary Taylor, one of the war's principal commanders. The Trenton *State Gazette*, however, agreed with Dayton, opining in September 1847 that "the territories to be annexed...will destroy the balance of the Union."

With the outbreak of hostilities, President Polk requested volunteer regiments from the states, including one from New Jersey, to supplement the small regular army. On May 22, 1846, New Jersey governor Charles C. Stratton called on "organized uniform companies and other citizens of the state to enroll themselves" in the regiment. Unfortunately, the enthusiasm of Jerseymen for actually fighting in the Mexican War proved, as in much of the Northeast, minimal. Although a number of existing volunteer militia companies allegedly offered to serve in the proposed regiment, all were well under minimum strength, and none could enlist the additional men required by the federal government. An angry Governor Stratton blamed New Jersey's failure on the "defective and prostrate condition of the militia system of the state." The following year, the federal government managed to recruit two small units in New Jersey: a four-company battalion of volunteers, which shipped out to Vera Cruz, and a three-company battalion to serve in the regular army's Tenth United States Infantry Regiment, which ended up stationed in Matamoros. Neither unit saw combat, although they both lost a number of men to disease and desertion.

Two of the most notable New Jersey veterans of the Mexican War were Robert Field Stockton and Stephen Watts Kearny, who cooperated and then clashed in California and played out their conflict on the national stage. Born in 1795, Stockton was, at one time or another, a wealthy aristocrat, heroic naval officer, monopoly capitalist, self-interested political operative, social progressive and apologist for slavery. In the course of all these twists and turns, he became one of the most influential and controversial men in New Jersey and, indeed, America in the first half of the nineteenth century. A grandson of Richard Stockton, New Jersey signer of the Declaration of Independence, and son of United States attorney, congressman and senator Richard Stockton, Robert attended the College of New Jersey (Princeton University) but discovered early on that adventure was more to his liking than scholarship and joined the navy as a midshipman in 1811. During the War of 1812, Stockton was cited for bravery and rose to the rank of lieutenant. In the postwar years, he challenged British naval officers to duels for not expressing sufficient respect for the American navy, fought Algerian and Caribbean pirates, captured illegal slave ships and, as the representative of the American Colonization Society, penetrated deep into West African rain forests and negotiated at pistol point with local chiefs to acquire what would become Liberia, planned as a homeland for freed African American slaves.

After a stint at the helm of the "Joint Companies," a New Jersey transportation monopoly composed of the Delaware and Raritan Canal

The explosion of Stockton's cannon aboard the *Princeton*. *NGMMNJ*.

and Camden and Amboy Railroad, Stockton returned to active naval service as a captain in 1838, subsequently met Swedish ship designer John Ericsson and brought him to America to design a steam-powered screw-propeller warship. Stockton supervised construction of the vessel, dubbed the *Princeton* in honor of his hometown and launched in Philadelphia in 1843. He personally designed one of its large guns, dubbed Peacemaker. On February 28, 1844, Captain Stockton took the *Princeton* for a cruise on the Potomac River, with President John Tyler, his cabinet and two hundred guests aboard. Peacemaker was successfully fired several times to entertain the guests, but then it exploded and killed six people, including Secretary of State Abel Upshur and Secretary of the Navy Thomas Gilmer.

The explosion that decimated Tyler's cabinet may have slowed Captain Stockton down a step or two, but he quickly recovered. The outbreak of the Mexican War in 1846 found him, an acting commodore, sailing north along the California coast aboard the USS *Congress* on a mission to reinforce Commodore John D. Sloat's American Pacific Squadron. On Stockton's arrival, the nervous and ailing Sloat, who had been nudging Mexican authorities in California toward accepting a peaceful American takeover, happily turned over command to the New Jersey officer. In a series of actions that earned him a reputation with one historian as "a competent seaman and an energetic officer" but also "vain, tactless, zenophobic [*sic*], and glory-thirsty," Stockton's aggressiveness undid Sloat's careful work, inciting a *Californio* rebellion. Aided by Brevet Captain John C. Fremont, an explorer who raised a ragtag force to conquer California, Stockton put together a little army, displayed his usual personal courage and revealed a surprising command of land-based tactical skills for a naval officer in battling the insurgents.

General Stephen Watts Kearny arrived in California right in the middle of the Stockton-inspired revolt. Kearny never achieved the notoriety of his naval counterpart and is far less well known than his storied nephew, Philip, one of the most famous Jerseymen of the century, who would lose an arm and become a hero in Mexico and gain more fame and glory before losing his life in the Civil War. Born in Newark in 1794, Kearny lived in that city and nearby New York for much of his life when not on active duty with the army in the West. In 1812, he left Columbia College to accept a commission as a first lieutenant in the Thirteenth United States Infantry. Promoted to captain in 1813, Kearny remained in the army at the close of the war. He was involved in the initial efforts to establish a military presence in the Louisiana Territory and accompanied several exploratory expeditions into what was then a little-known wilderness. Kearny commanded several of the first army posts beyond the Mississippi, including one at the site of Kearny, Nebraska, which was named for him. He was promoted to lieutenant colonel of the First United States Dragoons on the unit's formation in 1833 and elevated to the rank of colonel and command of that mounted regiment three years later.

With the outbreak of the Mexican War, Kearny was assigned to command the "Army of the West," a haphazard collection of Missouri mounted volunteer units, the Mormon Battalion and some artillery, stiffened by his own dragoon regiment, with orders to capture Santa Fe and move on to conquer California. Following an arduous overland march, Santa Fe fell to Kearny on August 18, 1846, without a shot being fired. After establishing a provisional government in New Mexico and leaving a garrison to secure the area, Kearny led three hundred dragoons on to fulfill his orders to conquer California. He encountered Kit Carson heading east on the trail and learned that California had already fallen to Stockton and Fremont and, unaware of the rebellion, sent two hundred of his men back to Santa Fe and continued west with the remainder. When Kearny reached San Pasqual, his diminished detachment of exhausted and bedraggled dragoons, mounted on played-out mules, encountered a superior force of *Californios* and lost eighteen men killed

Marker commemorating the battle of San Pasqual, California, in what is now a state park. *Wickimedia commons.*

in a brief but nasty fight. Fortunately for Kearny, Stockton and Fremont's ad hoc army of American adventurers, sailors and marines came to the rescue and joined forces with the dragoons to finally crush the mini-rebellion.

With the fighting over, Kearny considered his official orders from Washington to claim California for the United States as superseding the opportunistic actions of Fremont and Stockton—Stockton had arbitrarily named Fremont as governor of California—and advised them that he was now in charge. Stockton left for the east in a huff, more army troops arrived by ship and Kearny dismissed Fremont and assumed the title of governor himself. He then escorted Fremont back across the prairie to Fort Leavenworth, where he had him charged, court-martialed and convicted of mutiny and disobedience of orders. The court-martial sentenced Fremont to dismissal from the army. The captain's connections on high, including his father-in-law, Senator Thomas Hart Benton of Missouri, had the dismissal quashed, but Fremont resigned in anger. Following his California adventure, Kearny was appointed military governor of Vera Cruz, Mexico, until the peace treaty of Guadeloupe Hidalgo formally ended the Mexican War.

Kearny was awarded the brevet, or honorary, rank of major general for his wartime service and returned to his previous headquarters in Missouri. He died there on October 31, 1848, from yellow fever contracted in Mexico and was buried in Bellefontaine Cemetery in Saint Louis, far from his native Newark.

Following his vigorous but fruitless disagreement with Kearny over the reinstitution of California civil authority, Robert Stockton headed back east and left the navy. By 1848, segueing seamlessly into politics, he gave a speech in Philadelphia advocating complete annexation of Mexico. Stockton continued to play a role in state and national affairs until his death in 1866, serving briefly as a United States senator from New Jersey, offering himself as a potential presidential candidate to any party interested in 1856 and participating in a peace conference that attempted to head off the Civil War in early 1861, thus earning himself a permanent slot in the overflowing pantheon of colorful New Jersey characters.

CHAPTER 6

A "PECULIAR" HISTORY

THE TENTH NEW JERSEY INFANTRY IN THE CIVIL WAR

John Y. Foster, the first chronicler of New Jersey's Civil War units, noted that "the 10th Regiment had a history peculiar to itself." The regiment was raised by William Bryan as the "Olden Legion" in the late summer and fall of 1861. Bryan intended his legion to be a combined arms outfit, and the soldiers of one company were recruited as cavalrymen. Although named for New Jersey governor Charles Olden, the unit was not state-affiliated.

Colonel Bryan organized the legion at his hometown of Beverly, south of Trenton along the Delaware River. Sergeant Richard Love of Company C was not impressed by his unit's commanders, and wrote, "As military men, the least said about [Colonel Bryan and Lieutenant Colonel John W. Wright] the better." Love did concede that Major Matthew Berriman was "a persistent and hard worker (between drinks)."

The legion moved to Washington in December 1861, where it fell "almost immediately…into disrepute, owing to its defective organization and the absence of all proper discipline." In January 1862, the secretary of war requested Governor Olden to accept state responsibility for the hapless outfit—an offer the governor declined. When the secretary subsequently threatened to disband the unit if New Jersey didn't take it over, Olden, assured that he could name new officers, acquiesced. The governor dismissed Bryan, Wright and Berriman and appointed Colonel William Murphy as commander of the legion, which was redesignated the Tenth New Jersey Infantry Regiment. The new colonel instituted a regime of discipline and raised morale by enrolling the enlisted men for the monthly state stipend awarded to other New Jersey soldiers. Murphy also discharged the cavalry company's horseless horsemen and recruited an infantry company to replace them.

The Tenth New Jersey's internal problems spared its men the prospect of traveling to the Virginia Peninsula with Major General George B. McClellan's Army of the Potomac in the spring of 1862. While other Jerseymen struggled through the swamps around Richmond, the Tenth's new officers struggled to make the regiment a viable military organization. One of those officers was William H. Snowden, a former sergeant in the Third New Jersey Infantry, promoted to captain and command of the Cumberland County boys of Company D. Snowden, although competent, was a bit of a prig who felt "our volunteers can face bullets and bomb shells, and drive back armies, but they cannot withstand the subtle attacks of vice." He was impressed with Colonel Murphy, "a gentleman in every sense of the word," particularly since the colonel never engaged in the "almost universal, but debasing practice—profanity." He also approved of new Lieutenant Colonel William S. Truex, formerly the major of the Fifth New Jersey Infantry.

Improved discipline led to the Tenth's assignment to provost (military police) duty in Washington. Captain Snowden's company was assigned to patrol Georgetown, and he was quartered in the "comfortable rooms of a large secesh mansion." Private William S. Cazler of Company E, who worked as a clerk in a "Military Detective Prison" housing swindling government contractors and other offenders, thought Washington a "hole of filth and nuisance," but the soldiers of the Tenth led remarkably easy lives for Civil War soldiers. The enlisted men moved from tents into barracks, and one company actually resided in "a large brick house with a coal fire." Spit and polish, white gloves and good food and lodging continued to be the Tenth's lot in an increasingly sanguine war. Most of the regiment's men no doubt shared one soldier's sentiment that "the bloody Tenth has been wonderfully favored—peace be unto her bloodless victories." The formerly rowdy dissidents of

Captain William Snowden. *John Kuhl.*

the Olden Legion believed they would remain in Washington "as long as we behave ourselves and do our duty."

In March 1863, Colonel Murphy returned to New Jersey and was succeeded by Colonel Henry Ogden Ryerson of the Twenty-third New Jersey Infantry, a regiment due to be discharged in the summer. Ryerson, badly wounded at the battle of Gaines Mill in June 1862 while serving as a captain in the Second New Jersey Infantry, had commanded the Twenty-third at Fredericksburg and was an experienced and ambitious soldier. Offspring of a distinguished New Jersey family and a well-traveled attorney in civilian life, Ryerson had, unfortunately for the Tenth, a burning desire to be a general.

The delights of provost duty ended for the regiment in April 1863, when Colonel Ryerson received orders to lead his new command to Suffolk, Virginia, a Union foothold threatened by Confederate general James Longstreet's foraging force. The Tenth, which mustered seven hundred men for duty, was assigned to "Corcoran's Legion," a New York brigade raised by Irish American brigadier general Michael Corcoran. The previously pampered Jerseymen entered a world of "dig and delve, delve and dig, and picket duty, day and night, without ceasing," coupled with occasional reconnaissance marches.

On May 14, the 10th marched fifteen miles through a ruined landscape of burned and looted farmsteads to Carrsville, near the Blackwater River, where the regiment engaged in its first skirmish, losing three men wounded. Three days later, the Jerseyans marched out on another mission, which led to a friendly fire mishap due to a "bewildering confusion" when the horse of Colonel James P. McIvor of the 170th New York panicked and threw him. Several men were wounded in an exchange of fire between the two regiments. Following these minor excitements, the 10th settled down to garrison duty in unpleasant weather. Bored by the lack of action, Colonel Ryerson began to lobby to have his unit sent to a more active theater of war, noting that he longed for a "clash of arms." On July 2, 1863, as the battle of Gettysburg raged, the 10th packed up to move back North.

To Ryerson's disgust and his men's delight, the regiment was ordered to Philadelphia and then Pottsville, Pennsylvania, to enforce the military draft. The Jerseymen dubbed their outfit the "Excursion Regiment" as they subsequently moved through Reading, Carlisle and Chambersburg to Shepherdstown, Maryland, where they were deployed along the Potomac River. In November, the Tenth moved to Mauch Chunk (now Jim Thorpe) and Beaver Meadow, Pennsylvania, to back up local draft officials and suppress the draft-resisting Irish "Molly Maguires" across Carbon and

Luzerne Counties. An angry Colonel Ryerson viewed the miners as "treacherous, cowardly foreigners" and groused that he had "little chance for distinction or promotion."

The Jerseymen lived well in Pennsylvania, enjoying a Thanksgiving dinner of "roast beef, turkey, venison, bear steak and sour kraut." Over the winter, most of the Tenth's men, their service commitment due to expire in 1864, reenlisted, receiving large bounty payments and thirty day furloughs in return. The regiment also picked up a number of new recruits, all no doubt assured that they would serve out their enlistments in the hills of Pennsylvania. Ryerson, however, continued to badger higher headquarters with requests to send his regiment to the front. "I must have some change," he wrote, or "this life will kill me before long."

Unfortunately for his men, and, ultimately, himself, Ryerson got his wish, and his regiment was ordered to Virginia to join the Army of the Potomac's battle-hardened First New Jersey Brigade in the spring of 1864. On May 4, the men of the Tenth marched south to battle "with cheerful hearts and high hopes." Hope soon turned to horror, however, as General Robert E. Lee's Army of Northern Virginia attacked the Army of the Potomac in the underbrush of the Wilderness, and the Tenth was badly battered in the ensuing battle. On May 6, as the regiment laid down under heavy fire, Colonel Ryerson rose to his knees to assess the situation and was hit in the head by a bullet. Carried to a nearby cabin, he lingered without regaining consciousness until he died on May 12. In addition to Ryerson, the Tenth lost thirty-seven men killed, wounded and missing in the Wilderness.

Lieutenant Colonel Charles Tay led the Tenth out of the Wilderness and on to Spotsylvania, where he and a number of his men were captured in a mismanaged attack. The regiment finally marched away from that battlefield on May 21, leaving behind 149 men killed, wounded and missing. Colonel Tay

Lieutenant Colonel Tay was a "hard luck" commander because he got most of his regiment captured—twice! *John Kuhl.*

and the Tenth's POWs were liberated by Union cavalry raiders at Beaver Dam Station and rejoined the regiment in time to fight at Cold Harbor and then move on to Petersburg and the Shenandoah Valley, where on August 16, 1864, the Tenth, along with two other regiments of the First New Jersey brigade, fought a rear guard action along Abram's Creek, just south of Winchester. The outnumbered Jerseymen fell back to the town under cover of darkness, and Lieutenant Colonel Tay, once again confused by events, did not withdraw far enough. The regiment was surrounded and overrun, and Tay and 150 of his men became prisoners.

The August 16 fight effectively wrecked the Tenth New Jersey. The regiment, now a mere eighty men strong, was placed under the command of Major Lambert Boeman of the Fifteenth New Jersey. Although a shadow of its former self, the regiment fought well at Winchester and Fisher's Hill under Boeman's leadership. At the latter battle, the men of the Tenth, with Lieutenants John Wilson and Benjamin Pine in the lead, were the first Jerseymen to reach the Rebel lines. The two engagements cost the now tiny unit eighteen casualties.

When the Army of the Shenandoah was surprised in its camps by Confederate general Jubal Early's dawn attack at Cedar Creek on October

19, the steady Sixth Corps, which included the First New Jersey Brigade, saved the day by slowing the enemy advance. A timely New Jersey Brigade attack on the advancing enemy recovered several captured artillery pieces, but the Tenth lost another commander when Major Boeman was mortally wounded. The ranks of the regiment were severely thinned again, as forty-five of its men were killed and wounded.

The regiment returned to Petersburg with the Jersey Brigade in December 1864 and was reinforced by draftees, substitutes, volunteers, exchanged prisoners and men returning from the hospital. After several months

Major Lambert Boeman. *Wickimedia Commons.*

of trench duty, the Tenth took part in the Sixth Corps' April 2, 1865 breakthrough of the enemy lines. The following morning, a sharp-eyed private from the regiment spotted a white surrender flag flying from the Petersburg inner defense lines. The "Olden Legion" had fought its last fight.

The Tenth New Jersey spent the Appomattox Campaign guarding supply wagons and then did a stint of occupation duty along the North Carolina border before returning, now 450 men strong, to Washington with the Jersey Brigade, where it closed its peripatetic career on June 22, 1865, mustering out of service at Hall's Hill, Virginia, concluding a unique history that set it apart from all the other regiments the state sent to war.

CHAPTER 7

JERSEY BOYS TO THE RESCUE

As the spring turned into summer in 1864, the campaign ground down into a stalemate in the country south and east of Richmond. The heat became more oppressive and the Virginia chiggers burrowed beneath Yankee skin, doing their best to draw blood in defense of the "sacred soil." The landscape was familiar to the men of Company F, however, who were born and raised in the pine barrens of Ocean County, New Jersey. The gnarled pitch pines and scrub oak and the eerie cast of the moon on the sand roads at night were, in a curious way, a sort of homecoming, a sign that perhaps the war had come full circle and would soon be done.

But if things would be done here, they would be done without the help of Company F and its parent unit, the 14th New Jersey Volunteer Infantry Regiment, a unit raised in Mercer, Monmouth, Ocean, Middlesex and Union Counties in the summer of 1862. At 2:00 a.m. on July 6, 1864, the men of the 14th were awakened from their slumbers in the Petersburg siege lines and marched fifteen miles to City Point through a thick, lung-grabbing dust, which, coupled with the darkness, made it impossible to see more than a few feet. After reaching the point of embarkation at daybreak, the regiment was divided, part boarding the steamer *Columbia* with the 87th Pennsylvania Infantry, the remainder sharing *Sylvan Shore* with the 151st New York, sister units of the 14th in the First Brigade of the Third Division of the Army of the Potomac's 6th Army Corps.

And then the Jerseymen slid down the James, shedding the dust from their bodies and washing their clothes for the first time in two months. They passed Sloop Point and Hog Point and slipped out through Hampton Roads, where the *Monitor* had battled the *Virginia* to a draw two years before. As the transports nosed north into the broad expanse of Chesapeake Bay in daylight, it became clear that the whole Third Division was headed toward Washington and Baltimore. The boat ride was an idyllic interlude. While the officers totaled up the casualties since the spring campaign had begun in the Wilderness, the band of the Eighty-seventh Pennsylvania played "Maryland, My Maryland"—and that was where they were going.

The Third Division was shifted from the Petersburg lines to protect Washington, D.C., from a Rebel force under Lieutenant General Jubal Early. General Robert E. Lee had detached Early's corps from the Army of Northern Virginia and sent it to the Shenandoah Valley to drive out advancing Union troops and then seek opportunities to exploit in order to draw Union forces from the siege lines around Petersburg and relieve pressure on Lee's battered Army of Northern Virginia. After defeating the small federal army in the Shenandoah, Early continued to move north and crossed the Potomac into Maryland on July 5.

Most of Washington's defenders had been sent south to reinforce the Army of the Potomac under Lieutenant General Ulysses S. Grant and Major General George G. Meade, and Early seemed poised to either liberate thousands of Confederate prisoners of war held at Point Lookout on the Chesapeake or capture the capital—or both. His only opposition was a scratch force of several thousand men, predominantly militia and short service troops, under Major General Lew Wallace, who had consolidated his command along the Monocacy River in Maryland by the town of Frederick. On July 7, Wallace's men began to skirmish with advance elements of Early's corps. He hoped to hang on until reinforcements arrived, and much to his relief, they appeared in the form of Brigadier General James B. Ricketts's Third Division in the evening of July 8.

The area around Frederick was very familiar to the Jerseymen of the Fourteenth, as they had been stationed there to protect the railroad bridge across the Monocacy from Rebel raiders in 1862 and 1863. On the morning of July 9, while the regiment awaited the inevitable battle, several of the Fourteenth's officers, including First Brigade commander Colonel William S. Truex; Lieutenant Colonel Caldwell K. Hall, who assumed command of the regiment when Truex took over the brigade; and Major Peter Vredenburgh stopped by the Thomas family farm, which they had often visited when the Fourteenth was stationed along the Monocacy. The officers advised the family to evacuate the premises.

Colonel William Truex. *John Kuhl.*

As the day wore on, Union skirmishers fell back through the town of Frederick, crossed the river and assumed defensive positions. Wallace's command, including Ricketts's division, totaled less than six thousand men, who were deployed at several locations along the river as Early tentatively pushed his fourteen-thousand-man force forward.

The critical high ground on the Union side of the Monocacy was defended by the Sixth Corps men, with Ohio National Guardsmen on one-hundred-day duty guarding an upstream crossing at the "Jug Bridge." Early, who did not know the strength or quality of the force opposing him, sent a six-hundred-man cavalry force across the Monocacy at a shallow ford in the river to make contact with the federals and determine who they were. The Rebel horsemen dismounted and advanced in an infantry formation. Yankee skirmishers from the Third Division routed them with a blistering fire, and the Confederate commander realized he was facing more than the Maryland militia.

As his cavalry withdrew, Early ordered Major General John B. Gordon to take his division, a battle-tested infantry unit led by a competent commander, across the ford while Major General Stephen D. Ramseur pushed against a detachment of Vermonters holding the main bridge on the Third Division's right. An artillery duel began as the Fourteenth New Jersey and the other regiments of the First Brigade moved down to the now evacuated Thomas farm to confront Gordon.

Major Vredenburgh sat on his horse behind the Fourteenth New Jersey's main line and watched the Rebels coming on. At this stage of the war, he expected them to come running, dodging and diving, but to his amazement, they advanced as if on parade. Although Early had been suspicious of who he was opposing, he had apparently not conveyed that to Gordon, who probably thought his bold advance was directed at Maryland militiamen who would panic and run.

The Fourteenth held its fire until the enemy closed within 125 yards and then, along with the Eighty-seventh Pennsylvania, opened up with a deadly fusillade, killing both the colonel and lieutenant colonel of the Sixty-first Georgia Infantry and dropping a number of their men as the firefight broke out all along the Third Division line. Shortly afterward, Lieutenant Colonel Hall was hit in the wrist by an enemy bullet, which plowed up his arm and exited below his elbow. Hall staggered painfully to the rear and out of the war.

Color Sergeant William B. Cottrell, carrying the regiment's national flag, waved it back and forth to encourage the men until a bullet broke the staff and smacked into Cottrell's chest and he fell forward, bleeding all over the banner. It was picked up by Corporal George H. Bryan, who was shot and badly wounded himself. There would be revenge. Captain John C. Patterson tapped the shoulder of Private James Chafey of Hornerstown

Major Peter Vredenburgh. *John Kuhl.*

Lieutenant Colonel Caldwell Hall was badly wounded commanding the Fourteenth at Monocacy. *John Kuhl.*

and Company F and pointed to the Confederates in the ravine to the regiment's front. "Do you see that Rebel color?" yelled Patterson above the din, pointing at a Georgia battle flag. Chafey nodded. "Do you think you can lower it?" Chafey, a wild man in a fight who had distinguished himself at Cold Harbor the month before, shouted back, "I'll try." He ran to within thirty yards of the Confederate front, dropped to one knee, aimed his rifle-musket and did indeed bring down the color. His mission accomplished, Chafey scurried back to his own line, miraculously unharmed.

Captain James Conover of Company D, the Fourteenth's senior officer after Hall's departure, took command, only to be struck down almost immediately by a bullet in the thigh. Captain Chauncey Harris of Company C, next in the chain of command, was hit in the shoulder. Captain Symmes H. Stults and Captain Jacob J. Janeway were killed and wounded in quick succession. By then the Fourteenth had only three officers on their feet: Lieutenant Lemuel Buckelew, Captain Patterson and Lieutenant Samuel C. Baily—and then Buckelew was wounded. The toll among the officers was reflected in the ranks. Henry Havens, Patterson's first sergeant from Point Pleasant, was shot dead. Corporal Roderick Clark, also of Point Pleasant, a boat builder and

Left: Captain Jacob J. Janeway was killed in action at Monocacy. *John Kuhl.*

Right: First Lieutenant Lemuel Buckelew was wounded at Monocacy. *John Kuhl.*

"waterman" in civilian life, was hit by two bullets, one shattering his left leg below the knee and the other drilling through his right lung.

The outnumbered Third Division men began to fall back toward the Georgetown Pike. It was a fighting withdrawal, and the Jerseymen brought as many of the wounded with them as possible. Corporal Clark was not among those carried off. As he lay on the ground in the Thomas farmyard, what was left of the Georgians came on at a run, capturing a few Pennsylvanians not quick enough to leave the house. A Rebel threw himself down behind Clark's body and, using it as a rifle rest, fired at the retreating Yankees. Clark's face was scorched by the flash of gunpowder, and he was grazed by return fire that killed the Confederate.

Stretcher-bearers who began conveying the wounded to waiting ambulances were caught in a hail of enemy fire as well. Private Willis Haight of the 151st New York Infantry, detailed as a stretcher-bearer, was hit while carrying off Captain Conover. The slug struck the right side of Haight's head by his ear and passed out through his right eye. The twenty-two-year-old Niagara County farmer crumpled to the ground beside the wounded captain, and both were swirled up into the whirlwind of the Confederate charge. Captain Harris was shot again, in the leg, as he was being carried to an ambulance.

On reaching the Georgetown Pike, the Fourteenth and the other regiments of the First Brigade turned and faced the enemy once more and began to slug it out again. Corporal John Silvers, who had inherited the regiment's colors from the fallen Bryant, went down wounded. The flag, heavily flecked with Sergeant Cottrell's blood, was caught by seventeen-year-old veteran Tom Ryan, who raised it as a private and fell with it, his left leg broken, as a sergeant.

While the First Brigade fought for the Georgetown Pike, the Third Division's Second Brigade, deployed to its right, was pushed back as well, uncovering the partially burned bridge across the Monocacy, and Ramseur's Confederates stormed across to reinforce Gordon. The whole Third Division began to fall back again, and everyone who could carry a musket was called on to cover the retreat. Charlie Fleming, a sergeant in the Fourteenth who served in the brigade Pioneer (combat engineer) detachment, found himself back in the infantry and got shot through the right thigh to prove it. Charlie could still move, and took off limping toward Baltimore with the rest of the wounded.

The withdrawal continued as a deliberate retreat, not a rout, and the Yankees fell back fighting stubbornly. Sergeant Major William B. Ross of Freehold commanded the Fourteenth's rear guard and recalled later that as bullets zipped around him he felt twinges of immortality. Then his combat reverie was disturbed when he realized he was surrounded and away from his men, and he turned and ran two hundred yards to a woodlot, where he hid until his pursuers passed.

It was now 5:00 p.m. The Battle of Monocacy was over. Thanks largely to the Jersey boys and their fellow soldiers of the Third Division, General Wallace's command had inflicted enough damage on the enemy to prevent a pursuit. Many of the Union wounded, however, were left to lie on the field in ninety-degree heat. Some died there, but others were lucky. A slightly injured Confederate offered Corporal Clark a drink from his canteen. Sergeant Cornelius Barkalow of Company A, wounded in the chest, was recognized by a Confederate officer he had escorted as a prisoner back in 1862. Barkalow's generosity and kindness on that occasion paid dividends as he received prompt medical attention. Private James Taylor of Trenton, now a prisoner of war along with twenty-eight other Jerseyans from the Fourteenth, and the son of a mortician, may have reflected on his father's invention of a "convenient body cooler" as he surveyed the bloating corpses on the field.

The Fourteenth New Jersey lost heavily at the battle of Monocacy. There were about 350 men present with the regiment at the outset of the battle. On July 11, when the Fourteenth reassembled near Baltimore, the regiment mustered a mere five officers and ninety-eight enlisted men. Some, including Sergeant Major Ross, would rejoin the unit several days later, but twenty-four men were killed in action and another sixteen eventually died of wounds received at Monocacy. Other soldiers, seriously wounded like Corporal Clark, would spend the rest of the war in hospitals and be discharged for disability. In all, the Fourteenth lost more men killed and wounded, and fewer as prisoners, than any other Third Division regiment.

On Monday, July 11, Jubal Early's corps pushed up against the Federal forts northwest of Washington and found them

Private James Taylor of Trenton ended the battle a prisoner of war. *John Kuhl.*

Fourteenth New Jersey veterans at the dedication ceremony on July 11, 1907. *NGMMNJ.*

occupied by the First and Second Divisions of the Sixth Corps, which had arrived in the nick of time—time gained by the sacrifice of the Third Division. After probing the defenses of the capital, Early retreated. The Third Division later rejoined the rest of the Sixth Corps, pursuing the retreating Confederates into the Shenandoah Valley. In September and October 1864, as part of Major General Philip Sheridan's Army of the Shenandoah, the Fourteenth New Jersey would fight Jubal Early three more times. From Monocacy until the end of the war, the regiment would never be on the losing side in another battle.

Roderick Clark survived, minus a leg. He returned to Point Pleasant with a disability pension of eight dollars a month and went back to boat building. In 1879, he purchased a piece of property on the Manasquan

River and rented boats for fishing and crabbing to tourists as the Jersey shore became a resort area. Clark was active in veteran's affairs and was treasurer of a committee that raised money to erect a monument in 1907 to his regiment's fight at Monocacy. He outlived two wives and one of his children. The old soldier passed away on November 9, 1927, one of the last survivors of the Jersey Boys who helped save the capital on that bloody day in July 1864.

For more on the history of the Fourteenth New Jersey, see Bilby and Goble, Remember You Are Jerseymen.

CHAPTER 8

THE NEW JERSEY
NATIONAL GUARD GROWS UP:
1895–1921

In the last years of the nineteenth century and the first decade of the
twentieth, the New Jersey National Guard, a title assumed by the state's
militia in 1869, began to transition from a military-themed social and
political club occasionally called out by the governor in civil disturbances into
a more professional force. This trend, part of a national one, was fueled by
National Guard officers who wanted to gain respect from their regular army
counterparts as well as federal officials seeking a reliable organized backup
force for the regular army in an era of growing national responsibilities. The
first tentative steps in this direction began in the 1890s, with the assignment
of regular army officers to advise and train state forces. In 1895, the first
of these officers, Lieutenant Melvin W. Rowell of the Tenth United States
Cavalry, was assigned to the New Jersey National Guard.

At the outbreak of the Spanish-American War in 1898, the governor
of New Jersey received a request from the federal government to supply
three regiments of volunteer infantry for two years' service, as there was no
legal way to compel such service. In early May, National Guard regiments
reported to the state's training camp at Sea Girt, where they were requested
to provide volunteers and organize war-service units. There was no trouble
recruiting, for Guardsmen looked on the war as a great adventure. The First
Regiment was assigned to Camp Alger, Virginia, to guard supplies, and the
Second Regiment was sent to Jacksonville and then Pablo Beach, Florida.
One battalion of the Third Regiment was stationed at Pompton Lakes, New
Jersey, to guard the gunpowder factory there, and the other two battalions of

Governor Leon Abbett and his National Guard Staff at Sea Girt, circa 1890. *NGMMNJ.*

A battalion of the Third New Jersey Infantry was stationed at Pompton Lakes in 1898 during the Spanish-American War. *NGMMNJ.*

the Third garrisoned Fort Hancock on New Jersey's Sandy Hook peninsula as part of the New York Harbor defenses. In November, the entire Third Regiment moved to Athens, Georgia. A second call for troops produced a Fourth Regiment, which was ordered to Camp Meade, Pennsylvania, and then Greenville, South Carolina. No New Jersey regiment ever left the country, and all were discharged by February 1899.

The New Jersey Naval Militia was called to active duty and its men assigned to the regular navy fleet. Some of the state's sailors served on the blockading squadron off Cuba. Two Paterson African American men serving in the Tenth United States Cavalry, William H. Thompkins and George Wanton, were awarded the Medal of Honor for their courageous actions in rescuing members of a stranded reconnaissance party in Cuba. In 1921, Wanton served as an honorary pallbearer at the burial of the Unknown Soldier.

Although not awarded a medal, New Jerseyan Clara Louise Maas proved to be a real heroine in the Spanish-American War era. Newark-born Maas, an early graduate of the Newark German Hospital School of Nursing, became an army contract nurse during the war. While Maas was serving in Cuba in 1900, she volunteered to be bitten by a mosquito in an experiment in the effort to find a cure for yellow fever. She contracted the disease and died as a result. Maas's body was returned to Newark. where she was buried with military honors. In 1918, the Newark German Hospital was renamed Clara Maas Hospital in her memory.

Overall, National Guard performance in the Spanish-American War varied considerably from regular army standards, and in the wake of the conflict, Secretary of War Elihu Root was determined to reform and modernize the relationship between state and federal military forces. Root's ideas were codified in the Militia Act of 1903, also known as the "Dick Act" after its chief sponsor, Ohio congressman and National Guard officer Charles Dick.

The federal government had supplied firearms to state governments for militia use since the Militia Act of 1792, but the Dick act and subsequent legislation expanded funding to include other equipment, pay for expenses incurred in annual training and provide professional education for officers. In return, National Guard units were required to be structured according to regular army organizational standards and meet a federally specified schedule of training days. National Guard units that did not meet minimum strength specifications were to be disbanded, and the New Jersey adjutant general complained that the new standards "have tended to greatly retard recruiting." The War Department also extended direct federal control over the restructured state military organizations, which were now liable to be called directly into service by presidential order for periods of up to nine months of service.

The law also established two official classes of militia: the Reserve Militia, which included all able-bodied male citizens between the ages of eighteen and forty-five, making them subject to a draft in time of war, although they had no obligation in time of peace, and the Organized Militia, or National Guard units. This classification system was not uncommon in the states, but the Dick Act formalized and standardized it.

In 1908, the law was amended to remove the time restriction to a maximum of nine months of federal service but specified that federal service was for domestic duty only, since the U.S. attorney general had declared that foreign assignment of federalized National Guard units was unconstitutional. In 1916, with World War I raging in Europe, a new law provided a workaround to the overseas duty restriction by considering mobilized National Guardsmen as draftees into federal service. Although President Woodrow Wilson, a former governor of New Jersey, would run for reelection that fall on the slogan "he kept us out of war," it was clear to many that war was indeed in the offing.

The first mobilization of National Guard units under the new legislation occurred on June 19, 1916. The federal government ordered Guardsmen across the country, including three infantry regiments, one squadron of cavalry, two batteries of field artillery, one signal corps company, one field hospital and one ambulance company of the New Jersey National Guard, a total of 4,288 men, for duty on the Mexican border in the wake of the crisis caused by revolutionary leader Pancho Villa's raid into New Mexico. The units assembled at the National Guard Training Center at Sea Girt on June 21 and traveled from there to Douglas, Arizona, for border duty, where they remained for the rest of the year. According to one source, the Guardsmen returned to New Jersey disillusioned and demoralized by the experience. A number of officers resigned their commissions, many enlisted men declined to reenlist and few recruits seemed interested in National Guard Service.

Strange as it might seem to some people today, the possibility of entering the war in Europe, and the knowledge that the National Guard would be in the thick of the fighting, seems to have created a surge in Guard enlistments in early 1917. Following the April 6, 1917 American declaration of war on Germany, some elements of the New Jersey National Guard were mobilized to guard bridges, railroads and other critical sites. The Guard's engineer battalion was detailed to lay out Camp Dix, a massive new training center

New Jersey Guardsmen were ordered to Sea Girt in 1916 for duty on the Mexican border. *Joseph G. Bilby.*

Camp Dix in 1918. The camp was laid out and built by New Jersey National Guard engineers. *Joseph G. Bilby.*

New Jersey National Guard soldiers and their wives and sweethearts at Sea Girt during the World War I mobilization in 1917. *NGMMNJ.*

in the heart of the New Jersey Pinelands that would boast 1,600 buildings within a year.

The remainder of the New Jersey National Guard was mobilized at Sea Girt on July 25 and formally inducted into United States service on August 5. Most of the 9,285 New Jersey Guardsmen left for Anniston, Alabama, shortly afterward, where they were assigned to the Twenty-ninth Division, organized at Camp McClellan from New Jersey, Maryland and Virginia National Guard units in late August. The Twenty-ninth became known as the "Blue and Gray Division" because it included National Guardsmen from states that had opposed each other during the Civil War. The name inspired the division's distinctive insignia patch, a yin and yang or "tae guk" combination featuring blue and gray elements.

Although most New Jersey National Guard units ended up in the Twenty-ninth Division, the ambulance company from Red Bank was assigned to the Forty-second "Rainbow" Division. The Naval Militia Brigade, some 401 men from Newark, Jersey City and Camden, was absorbed by the U.S. Navy.

The New Jersey units gained new federal designations. For example, the former 1st, 2nd and 4th New Jersey Infantry Regiments were combined to form the new 114th U.S. Infantry Regiment, while other state units were merged to create the 113th Infantry Regiment. Both regiments and other New Jersey units became the 29th Division's 57th Infantry Brigade. The Red Bank company became the 42nd Division's 165th Ambulance Company.

In June and July 1918, the Twenty-ninth Division landed in France. After spending time training in relatively quiet areas of the western front, the division moved to a "Defensive Sector" in Alsace for more advanced training under enemy fire and then, in September, joined the main American army for the Meuse-Argonne offensive. Beginning on October 8, the division engaged in twenty-one straight days of combat, advanced over four miles, captured 2,500 prisoners and lost one-third of its strength. Following the end of hostilities on November 11, the Twenty-ninth remained in France until receiving orders to return home on April 6, 1919. The division sailed for the United States between May 6 and 12. Separate units arrived in Newport News, Virginia, and Hoboken between May 14 and 25 and assembled at Fort Dix to be mustered out of service.

Donald McGowan of Orange had just graduated from high school when he went off to the Mexican border in 1916. By 1918, he was the sergeant major of the 114th Infantry Regiment in France. McGowan commanded the 102nd Cavalry in the 1944 Normandy invasion and rose to the rank of major general and chief of the army division of the National Guard Bureau in Washington before retiring in 1963. *NGMMNJ/Jay McGowan.*

Many New Jerseyans, draftees from civilian life, served in other units during the war, particularly the Seventy-eighth division, organized at Camp Dix of draftees primarily from New York and New Jersey. An estimated 130,000 to 150,000 New Jerseyans served in all branches of the armed forces in World War I, and 3,836 died from combat, accidents and disease, particularly influenza.

The return of the 113th Infantry to New Jersey in 1919. *NGMMNJ.*

The Twenty-ninth division was mustered out of federal service at Camp Dix in May 1919. Under the terms of their technically being "drafted," the New Jersey National Guardsmen who served in the Twenty-ninth were discharged not back to state duty but from military service entirely. The militia units New Jersey raised during the war to replace the Guard in state service were disbanded in January 1920, and the New Jersey National Guard, which effectively no longer existed, subsequently began to reorganize, with new units carrying the lineage of the old prewar units but now using federal designations reflecting Twenty-ninth Division service.

By the mid-1920s, the New Jersey National Guard had evolved into a modernized military organization that was an integral part of the nation's defense system. Within two decades, it would be called on again, as America geared up for World War II. It would not be found wanting.

For further reading, see Cooper, The Rise of the National Guard, *and Cutchins,* Twenty-Ninth Division.

CHAPTER 9

BLACK TOM AND KINGSLAND

THE JERSEY MOSQUITOES WERE NOT TO BLAME

O n the steamy summer night of July 30, 1916, a groggy young Tom Carroll awoke on his bedroom floor, tossed there by a shock wave that reverberated through his house in the wake of a thunderous explosion that rolled into a symphony of shattering glass and barking dogs that resonated through Carroll's Bayonne, New Jersey neighborhood. A series of smaller secondary explosions continued for some time afterward, and when Carroll cautiously peeked out a broken window, he saw a street full of curious and frightened neighbors gazing skyward in the direction of Jersey City at what appeared to be a fireworks display. Seventy years later, he vividly recalled his experience that hot July night as perhaps the most memorable of his life.

The effects of the massive explosion that awakened Carroll were felt far beyond the streets of Bayonne, rumbling through New Jersey, New York and Pennsylvania as far south as Philadelphia with the impact of an earthquake measuring 5.5 on the Richter scale. It all began when a mysterious blaze broke out aboard a boat docked at the Black Tom Island pier in Jersey City. The fire quickly spread to and detonated trainloads of ammunition awaiting overseas shipment along the wharf, which was the Lehigh Valley Railroad's Jersey City freight terminal. Over the previous two years, the terminal had evolved into a major staging area for American-made munitions being exported to Europe for use by the Allies fighting Germany during World War I.

With daylight came an assessment of the full scope of the disaster. All structures in a wide radius adjacent to the wharf and rail yard were

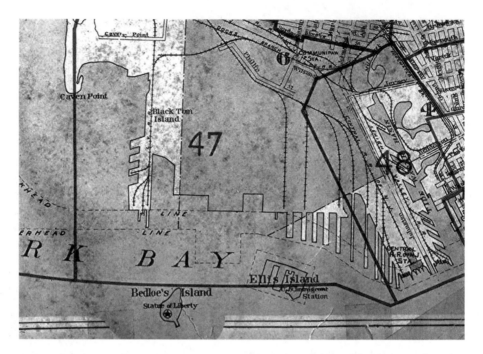

A map showing the location of Black Tom Island in relation to the immigration station on Ellis Island and Bedloe's Island, location of the Statue of Liberty. *James M. Madden.*

obliterated, and windows were smashed in all directions for a considerable distance, including across the Hudson River on Wall Street in Manhattan. Seven-year-old Margaret Geoghegan would remember the explosion in the distance that rattled the windowpanes in her tenement apartment on Sixty-first Street between Amsterdam and Columbus Avenues for the rest of her life. Telephone poles were toppled and buildings damaged to a greater or lesser degree throughout Jersey City and neighboring towns, not only from the force of the blast but also by shrapnel from exploding shells and flying debris that showered down from the deadly fireworks display illuminating the night sky.

Black Tom Island (actually by 1916 a peninsula connected by landfill to the shore) jutted out into New York Bay just behind America's iconic symbol— the Statue of Liberty on Bedloe's Island. Buildings around the statue were heavily damaged, with roofs ripped off and holes punched in walls by a rain of iron bolts, shells, spikes, shrapnel and chains tossed willy-nilly into the air by the explosion. The statue itself was relatively unscathed, save for a slightly torn gown and some shrapnel punctures in her upraised arm, which was

Destruction of the ammunition pier in the aftermath of the Black Tom explosion. *James M. Madden.*

then closed to visitors. Her pedestal, a former War of 1812 fort constructed to withstand high impact cannon fire, took the brunt of the blast, and the main entrance to the statue, a four-inch-thick iron door, was wrenched off its hinges and crushed inward as if by a giant hand. The minimal damage to Lady Liberty herself was widely interpreted as a symbolic testament to her role as a monument to freedom. The United States would use the statue's image extensively in the wartime years ahead, in recruiting posters as well as Liberty Bond drives to support the war financially.

Ellis Island, the nearby site of the New York immigrant receiving and processing station, was also bombarded with debris and was described as having the appearance of a war-torn village, with every window in every building shattered, the terra-cotta roof of the hospital collapsed and broken glass and shrapnel, along with unexploded three-inch-shells, tossed from across the water by the blast, strewn everywhere. Terrified immigrants on the island were quickly evacuated to lower Manhattan.

A. Harry Moore, Jersey City's commissioner of parks and public buildings (and a future New Jersey governor), reported that Jersey City's historic city hall, a mile away from the blast, was shaken to its foundations, suffering cracked walls and buckled floors. The floor of city hall's ornate council chamber was covered with debris from the shattered ceiling. Damage throughout the region was later assessed at an estimated $20 million in 1916 dollars.

Fortunately, the Black Tom terminal was not located in a residential area, and the late hour of the blast also limited potential injuries. Remarkably, although some have asserted that as many as seven people were killed, only four deaths have been identified, including a railroad guard at the terminal, a Jersey City child thrown from its crib by the shock wave and Jersey City policeman James Dougherty, who was patrolling the area at the time and was fatally injured by flying metal splinters. The fourth fatality was the captain of the barge where the initial fire broke out, reported missing until his body washed ashore six weeks later.

Ever eager to exploit a marketing opportunity, Jersey City merchants attempted to capitalize on the disaster by placing eye-catching slogans in their newly replaced windows in the days that followed. The *Jersey Journal* for

Shells from Black Tom landed miles away, and this young lady "souvenir hunter" found a few. *James M. Madden.*

July 31 informed its readers that one such sign read: "The explosion blows in my windows, you come in and blow yourself in a new suit." Another store informed shoppers that "Allies' dynamite smashed our windows: we smashed our prices." Hoboken ferry officials reported that they were intercepting entrepreneurial souvenir hunters carrying unexploded shells and pieces of shrapnel across the Hudson to New York to sell them.

Post-explosion investigations went in several directions. Jersey City public safety commissioner (and soon-to-be mayor) Frank Hague, no friend to the under-taxed railroads that crisscrossed his city, did not offer an explanation for the detonation but accused the president of the Lehigh Valley Railroad of violating a specified time limit for storing dynamite at the terminal, asserting that the railroad was thus responsible for placing public safety in jeopardy. Two watchmen were arrested and accused of starting the fire that detonated the munitions by carelessly positioning burning smudge pots to ward off the legendarily voracious New Jersey marsh mosquitoes.

More serious investigations led to the release of the watchmen and the conclusion that German saboteurs, attempting to halt or at least slow the shipments of war material to Great Britain and France, were at the root of the Black Tom disaster. Michael Kristoff, a Slovak ironworker living with relatives in Bayonne, was subsequently arrested and confessed that he had assisted some German agents in moving what appeared to be explosives to the terminal area. The actual devices seem to have been specialized incendiary time-delayed "pencil bombs" or "cigar bombs." Various other assertions were made alleging collusion with the Irish *Clan na Gael* revolutionary movement and even an Indian independence group, but there seems little doubt in retrospect that the actual event was initiated by German saboteurs.

Evidence suggesting German involvement led to a reevaluation of other mysterious fires and explosions that had occurred at New Jersey plants and factories contracted to supply the Allied forces. The incidents included a May 3, 1915 explosion at the Anderson Chemical Plant in Wallington that killed three people, as well as a series of fires and explosions at the John A. Roebling's Sons steel plant in Trenton and a January 10, 1916 explosion at the DuPont Gunpowder Factory at Carneys Point on the Delaware River that killed five workers. There had also been suspicious derailments of trains carrying munitions across New Jersey to ports of departure.

Barring conclusive evidence, some of these incidents were considered the result of accidents or sabotage by disgruntled employees rather than German agents, but it was clear that there had been a rash of mysterious

Black Tom shells dredged up out of the Hudson River after the explosion. *Library of Congress.*

disasters at New Jersey factories that had war material contracts with Britain, France and Russia. The factories were easy potential targets for German saboteurs, who could blend in with the large New Jersey immigrant labor force that performed risky jobs for poor pay and was not well screened prior to employment. Most of the factories also had inadequate emergency plans to handle disasters should they occur.

On one occasion, an ad hoc emergency plan was enacted by a single individual who kept her head in the presence of chaos. Six months after Black Tom, another massive explosion occurred across the meadowlands just over seven miles from Jersey City at a forty-acre ammunition manufacturing plant operated by the Canadian Car and Foundry Company in Kingsland and exporting its production to Russia. On January 11, 1917, a fire broke out at a worker's bench in a building that prepared shells for cleaning and loading the shells with gunpowder and quickly spread throughout the plant buildings as well as to nearby ammunition-filled railroad cars waiting to leave for Jersey City. The fire initiated a four-hour-long daisy chain of explosions as hundreds of thousands of shells either detonated or were thrown into the air, causing over $17 million dollars worth of damage. Twenty-five-year-old telephone operator Theresa "Tessie" McNamara, the first woman hired by the company, became a heroine that day. Tessie stayed at her post, calling not only the fire and police departments but all forty buildings in the complex as well, warning workers to evacuate immediately.

Tessie McNamara's subsequent account of her actions that day is a testament to her courage: "My first thought was to save the lives of the 1,700 men in the buildings. While making my calls, the first shell struck the building and passed about five feet from where I was sitting. About a dozen buildings were now on fire, and I had completed all calls. I started to leave the building without a coat, but I couldn't walk. My courage left me and the arriving firemen picked me up, wrapped a big coat around me and rushed for the gate."

The plant was completely destroyed, and the houses overlooking it from a nearby hill, many of them occupied by the company's largely immigrant workforce, were damaged or destroyed. A number of homes in neighboring Rutherford were struck by flying shells, and a car the police chiefs of Kingsland and Rutherford were riding in was hit by a three-inch round, which destroyed their automobile but left them unscathed. Fortunately, most

Shells from both Black Tom and Kingsland flew miles from the sites of the explosions. This one, from Kingsland, ended up in a railroad tie two miles away. *James M. Madden.*

of the shells in the plant had not yet been fitted with fuses, so they did not explode on landing. Remarkably, not a single life was lost to the disaster.

During the subsequent investigation, it was determined that the fire that led to the explosions had begun at the work station of Theodore Wozniak, who had served in the Austro-Hungarian army prior to the war. Efforts to find and question Wozniak failed, as he disappeared, leaving suspicions that Kingsland, like Black Tom, was a case of sabotage.

There would be several more explosions in New Jersey factories during the course of World War I. The most significant of these occurred on October 4, 1918, when the T.A. Gillespie Shell Loading Plant, located in the Morgan section of Sayreville, exploded, destroying the munitions manufacturing operation and setting off three days of detonations that destroyed more than three hundred buildings in Sayreville and South Amboy. Sayreville, South Amboy and Perth Amboy were evacuated and martial law temporarily established. Over one hundred people are estimated to have perished. It was generally agreed that Morgan was the result of an accident.

An extensive postwar investigation uncovered evidence that a network of German spies had indeed operated within the United States both before and during the war, and an international lawsuit, claiming that both the Black Tom and Kingsland explosions were the result of sabotage, was filed against Germany. In 1930, a German American Mixed Claims Commission decided against the United States and the lawsuit claimants, including the Lehigh Valley Railroad, the Canadian Car and Foundry Company and others, clearing Germany of any responsibility. The commission report essentially blamed the New Jersey mosquitoes for Black Tom, citing that the employees who had deployed the smudge pots had in fact ignited the boxcars loaded with shells. Despite the decision, the claimants did not give up and continued to press their argument for sabotage.

In 1939, the Claims Commission met again to reconsider the case, this time without German participation. It ruled that the Germans had presented fraudulent information during the initial investigation and awarded $50 million to the American claimants. World War II intervened, and final arrangements for payment did not occur until a 1953 agreement with the Federal Republic of Germany, which never admitted German responsibility but agreed to pay $50 million dollars in damages to the claimants from both explosions. Payment was finally made in 1979.

Today, the remains of Black Tom wharf are part of Liberty State Park, and most visitors are no doubt unaware of the 1916 explosion as they take in a striking view of the Statue of Liberty with a backdrop of the Manhattan

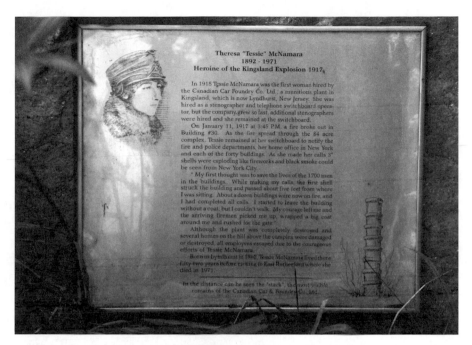

Above: Plaque dedicated to Tessie McNamara, heroine of Kingsland at the site of the disaster. *James M. Madden.*

Right: All that remains of the ammunition plant at Kingsland is this chimney. *James M. Madden.*

skyline, although an often-overlooked historic marker explains the story. Another fact largely unknown to visitors to the statue is that the lack of public access to the viewing area originally built into the torch dates from 1916. It was never reopened after closure in the immediate aftermath of the Black Tom disaster, one of the worst acts of terrorism in the United States prior to September 11, 2001.

Although an industrial park off Clay Avenue in Lyndhurst abuts the old Canadian Car Company property, the site of the 1917 Kingsland ammunition plant has mostly been reclaimed by the New Jersey Meadowlands. Recent efforts to mark the location have resulted in a small park with an observation platform, used mostly by birders, that provides a view of the area and a lone smoke stack rising out of the swamp—the sole surviving evidence of a building that got an evacuation call from Tessie McNamara. A plaque at the foot of the platform commemorates Tessie's heroism in a long-forgotten tale of New Jersey's role in the War to End All Wars.

For more on Black Tom, see Millman, The Detonators and Witcover, Sabotage at Black Tom. *For more on Kingsland, see "The Kingsland Explosion," by the Lyndhurst Historical Society (http://lyndhursthistoricalsociety.org/KingslandExplosion.html). The subsequent Morgan explosion is covered thoroughly in Gabrielan,* Explosion at Morgan.

Chapter 10

"HEAVEN, HELL OR HOBOKEN"

As World War I raged in Europe in the years following 1914, the United States remained officially neutral. Despite its noncombatant status, however, the country supported the Allied forces fighting the Central Powers with sales of military hardware. Major American firearms manufacturing companies, including Winchester and Remington, made rifles for the British, French and Russians, and other factories churned out ammunition and explosives from rifle cartridges to artillery shells and bombs. New Jersey, as one of the country's foremost industrial states, was home to a significant number of those plants, and the Imperial Russian government established an ammunition testing facility in Lakehurst.

President Woodrow Wilson, a former New Jersey governor, predicated his 1916 reelection campaign (headquartered in Asbury Park) on the slogan "he kept us out of war" and gained a narrow victory over Republican opponent Charles Evans Hughes. The subsequent revelation of the contents of the disconcerting Zimmermann Telegram, in which Germany was encouraging Mexico into an alliance against the United States, pushed the country closer to intervening in the conflict, however, and the German declaration of unrestricted submarine warfare on the open seas proved the final straw. The United States declared war on Germany on April 6, 1917.

The New Jersey city of Hoboken, which became the main port of embarkation for the American Expeditionary Force (AEF) army, was a vital cog in the American war effort. More than 1.5 million of the over 2 million soldiers who left the United States for the war in Europe boarded

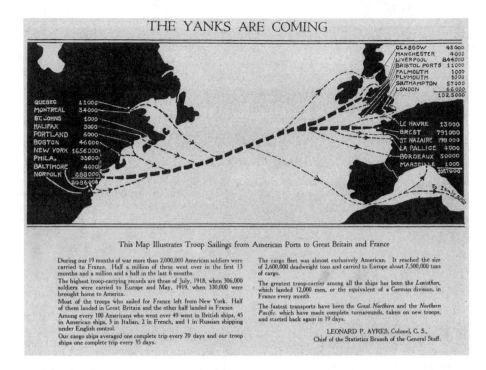

A map showing the number of soldiers sent to Europe in World War I and where they shipped out from. The designation of "New York" as a port means Hoboken. *Joseph G. Bilby.*

troop transports in the city. Situated across the Hudson River from New York City (and thus considered part of the port of New York for army purposes), Hoboken was already a major transoceanic cargo and passenger transportation hub, and following the declaration of war, the federal government seized existing German shipping company piers, warehouses and vessels, including the Hamburg-America luxury liner *Vaterland*, which was renamed *Leviathan* and turned into a troop transport, all along the city's waterfront.

Hoboken's culture was transformed by the advent of war. Long known as "Little Bremen" due to the large number of German immigrants who had settled there since the mid-nineteenth century, the city had continued to attract migrating Germans into the twentieth century. Hoboken was distinguished by its German specialty shops, social clubs and beer halls, reflecting an enduring Teutonic heritage. With the outbreak of war, many recent German immigrants living in the city were classified as enemy aliens prohibited from residing close to military facilities and were transported to Ellis Island. A nationwide general climate of mistrust toward German Americans was created deliberately by George Creel's United States Committee on Public Information, a government agency founded to foment anti-German sentiment among the American people. Creel's work led to sauerkraut relabeled as "liberty cabbage," dachshunds becoming "liberty pups" and German Valley, New Jersey, being renamed Long Valley, among other absurdities. His committee's propaganda-induced paranoia was buttressed by actual events, including a series of unexplained munitions plant and depot explosions, most notably Black Tom Island, a few miles south of Hoboken in Jersey City, which occurred prior to American entry into the war.

Hoboken became a military town, with soldiers patrolling the streets on the lookout for enemy sympathizers among the German American population. In addition, the army, setting the stage for postwar Prohibition, initially demanded that local saloons surrounding the embarkation piers be closed so that soldiers were not tempted to imbibe before boarding ships and then upped the ante by insisting that taverns within a half-mile radius of the docks be closed and that those beyond that distance close by 10:00 p.m. every night. The city fathers resisted these last demands, allowing bars to stay open well past the designated hour. Eventually, a compromise was reached, but by then, many of Hoboken's traditional watering holes had shut down due to loss of business.

Local people quickly became aware that young soldiers were interested not only in alcohol but also in female companionship. One newspaper reported that due to the rising population of transient military men in the city, six society women had volunteered to serve without pay patrolling the Hoboken streets at night, intercepting young ladies seeking adventure and escorting them back to their parents. The army did not look upon this situation lightly either and made efforts to round up single women walking the streets after dark and have them charged with prostitution.

Soldiers not only shipped out overseas from Hoboken but also passed through the port on the way home. The first returning soldiers were, however, deceased. Prior to the end of hostilities on November 11, 1918, men who were killed in action or lost their lives due to other causes overseas were buried where they died. That policy changed after the armistice, and Hoboken's Pier Number 4 warehouse on River Street was converted into a funeral chapel and morgue. Many of the dead were casualties from Archangel in Russia, where American soldiers supported White Russian forces fighting the Bolsheviks after the formal end of hostilities on the western front. The

Bodies of American Soldiers Brought From Russia

AMBULANCES CONTAINING BODIES OF 103 AMERICAN SOLDIERS WHO PERISHED IN THE ARCHANGEL CAMPAIGN ON WAY TO TEMPORARY RESTING PLACE.

CASKETS CONTAINING BODIES OF AMERICAN SOLDIERS ON HOBOKEN PIER.

Coffins bearing the remains of soldiers who died in Russia land in Hoboken. Americans were stationed in Russia, supporting the anti-Bolshevik forces, through 1920. *James M. Madden.*

first of these morgue vessels, the *Lake Daraga*, known popularly as the "ship of death," pulled into port flying a black pennant on the bow to announce its doleful cargo. Flags along the waterfront were dropped to half-mast and the sound of taps resonated through the air as metal coffins shrouded with American flags were disembarked with full military honors before being shipped home. The scene was replayed a number of times in 1919.

In 1918, General John Pershing, predicting a quick end to the war, allegedly promised his men they would be "home by Christmas." Soldiers entering battle on the western front that year translated their near-future prospects into the more graphic slogan "heaven, hell or Hoboken." The port of

This page and next: Soldiers in the streets of Hoboken. *James M. Madden.*

Hoboken and its allied site, nearby Camp Merritt, thus came to symbolize safe home to the men of the AEF. About as many homeward-bound soldiers landed in Hoboken as had left on the way to war—the total, coming and going, approaching three million.

VIPs passed through Hoboken as well, including President Wilson on his way to and from the Paris Peace Conference aboard the USS *George Washington*. On his return to New Jersey in July 1919, Wilson told cheering local citizens how homesick he had been while abroad and referred to Hoboken as "a beautiful city." A military band from Camp Merritt serenaded the president from the pier as hundreds of schoolgirls and other spectators greeted his arrival. Prominent local politicians, including Hoboken mayor Patrick Griffin, Jersey City mayor Frank Hague, Hudson County state senator and future governor Edward I. Edwards, as well as a bevy of other county

Democratic Party leaders, attended the ceremonies, providing the president with visual reminders of their continuing support.

Long-forgotten Camp Merritt played as big a role as Hoboken in World War I. As the Hudson River city morphed into a military port, the army realized that a nearby staging area was needed to house the vast number of troops who would be passing through on their way to Europe. Planners surveyed nearby rural areas situated near convenient transportation links to Hoboken and selected a 770-acre site in northern Bergen County, a location that had been considered for a camp during the Spanish-American War. The camp was laid out on land within the town limits of Cresskill, Dumont, Haworth and Demarest, located between the Hudson and Hackensack Rivers on high ground a few miles from the Palisades. The location was optimal, with access to the Northern and West Shore railroad lines as well as river transport down the Hudson, and it had access to a large enough water supply to accommodate a small city, which is what the camp became.

Camp construction was initiated on August 17, 1917, and the first troops began arriving on October 1. The center of Camp Merritt was located near the intersection of today's Knickerbocker Road and Madison Avenue in the borough of Cresskill. Originally designed to accommodate 28,881 personnel at a time, Camp Merritt's housing capacity was increased twice

An aerial view of Bergen County's Camp Merritt in 1918. *NGMMNJ.*

to accommodate 45,065 men, although it is believed that even more soldiers were crammed into its barracks on a number of occasions. The camp contained a total of 1,302 buildings, including barracks, administrative buildings, hospitals, warehouses, garages and other structures.

Unlike Camp Dix in Burlington County, Camp Merritt was never designed to be a training post. Its only mission was to serve as a temporary destination where soldiers who had trained in other areas of the country were held for no more than ten days before moving on to Hoboken and shipping out to the battlefields of Europe. The camp was named for Wesley Merritt, a New Yorker who graduated from West Point in 1860. Merritt was an exceptional officer who rose rapidly in rank during the Civil War. He commanded a cavalry brigade during the Gettysburg Campaign and was one of the officers who received the surrender of the Army of Northern Virginia in 1865. Merritt subsequently served on the frontier, was superintendent of West Point, commanded United States ground forces in the Philippines during the Spanish-American War as a major general and served as governor general of the Philippines. He died in 1910 and was buried at West Point.

In 1918, Camp Merritt, often called the "goodbye camp" by departing soldiers, was the final stop where wives, sweethearts and parents could come to visit and bid farewell to men departing for overseas. A local pastor was reportedly kept busy marrying blissful brides to their soon-to-be-departing grooms, and one camp volunteer mused that the minister scarcely had time to say his prayers due to his intense nuptial performance pace. The formerly quiet, rural Bergen County countryside around Camp Merritt resounded with the noise and bustle of bands and troops on the march, moving in and out of the camp at an increasingly feverish pace, as Merritt played out its critical role in the war effort. Merritt was also the "welcome home camp," like Hoboken, as many soldiers passed through its gates on their way home as on their way overseas.

Local Bergen County organizations, including the YMCA, Knights of Columbus, Jewish Welfare Board and the American Library Association, were active in supporting the transient soldiers at Camp Merritt and providing them with little luxuries from books and games to chocolate candy. In January 1919, soldiers from the camp visited all of the schools in Bergen County, handing out thirty-seven thousand medals inscribed "The Boys of Camp Merritt are grateful to you" to the students as a means of expressing their gratitude to the local community.

Camp Merritt, like the army itself, was not racially integrated, but both white and African American soldiers were housed in fairly close quarters there

Soldiers from Camp Merritt marching down to the dock at Alpine to board a boat for Hoboken. *Joseph G. Bilby.*

for brief periods of time. Although it existed in a racially charged era as Jim Crow took full hold in the South and African Americans began to demand their full rights as citizens, racial conflict appears to have been minimal at the camp, save for one tragic incident. White soldiers from Mississippi sent a threatening letter to the local YMCA secretary demanding that black soldiers not be allowed to enter a YMCA building they wished reserved for white men. On August 18, 1918, after the secretary declined to accede to their demands, twenty-five Mississippians marched into the YMCA building and forcibly ejected five African Americans. Black soldiers who gathered to protest the ejection and assert their right to go wherever they wished then faced off against a group of southern white troops. Rumors of razor fights and other atrocities spread on both sides, and as the situation verged on a full-scale riot, military police finally moved in and broke up the hostile crowds with swinging nightsticks. Several shots were fired in the course of the ensuing mêlée. Two black soldiers were wounded, and a third, Private Edward Frye of Kentucky, who was not involved in the disturbance and was sitting in his barracks, was killed when a stray bullet hit him in the chest.

Postcard images show African American soldiers at Bergen County's Camp Merritt. *James M. Madden.*

By the end of 1919, with all the wartime soldiers discharged, Camp Merritt was decommissioned and began to be disassembled, and the few remaining troops on the premises were transferred to Camp Dix. Many of the abandoned camp buildings were subsequently destroyed in several "mysterious" fires. Enterprising builders, eyeing the advantages of the site's proximity to New York City, then swooped in to buy up land, the remaining buildings and lumber, transforming the former military base into commuter cottages. Many still-standing houses constructed in this area of Bergen County during the 1920s have frames of Camp Merritt wood.

On Memorial Day, May 30, 1924, a sixty-five-foot obelisk was dedicated in Cresskill to commemorate Camp Merritt, the troops stationed there and, most importantly, the fifteen officers, four nurses, 558 enlisted men and one civilian who died, mostly from influenza, while serving their county

The Camp Merritt monument today. *James M. Madden.*

The base of the Camp Merritt monument today. *James M. Madden.*

there. New Jersey governor George S. Silzer presided over the ceremony, and General Pershing was the guest of honor. Twenty thousand spectators, including Major General Merritt's widow, who unveiled the monument, were in attendance.

Some of the present roadways around the 1924 monument are the original streets laid out by the army, silent witnesses to the long-ago tramp of doughboys on their way to Hoboken and the fields and trenches of France. Newer neighborhood streets—including Pershing Place; Stivers Street, named for Lieutenant Colonel D. Gay Stivers, the quartermaster officer who established the camp; and Merritt Avenue—bear witness to the World War I heritage of the area. Merritt Memorial Elementary School and Merritt Field also assure that no matter the dramatic changes in the landscape, the memory of Camp Merritt, however faded, will endure.

Hoboken's waterfront has also changed dramatically from the rough-and-tumble World War I–era docks of a century ago into a cityscape of gentrified brownstones, exclusive retail shops, offices and luxury high-rises with million-dollar views of Manhattan. The only vestiges of the city's role in World War I are two monuments near the river. One, a memorial plaque dedicated by the Knights of Columbus in 1925 mounted on a boulder at the foot of First Street, commemorates the travels of the AEF from Hoboken to Europe and back. The other, a bronze statue of a soldier and a marine welcomed home by a girl bearing flowers and a dog, was erected in 1922 in Elysian Park as a tribute to the city's servicemen rather than Hoboken's greater role in the war. Both provide mute and enduring testimony to the men who served in a conflict that was supposed to be "the war to end all wars" but, unsurprisingly, wasn't.

For more on Hoboken and Camp Merritt in World War I, see Gabrielan, Hoboken; *Johnson,* Heaven, Hell or Hoboken; *Dunn, "Merritt Dispatch"; Johnson, "Camp Merritt"; and Ziegler-McPherson,* Immigrants in Hoboken.

CHAPTER 11

ON THE ROAD TO WAR ONCE MORE

With the wholesale draft of its men into federal service on August 5, 1917, America's National Guard, including that of New Jersey, officially ceased to exist. The state had begun to raise several new units of field and coast artillery for its Guard following the declaration of war that April, but they were not completely organized or inspected by the date of the federal draft and so remained in state service. These units were never fully organized, although they were still technically part of the New Jersey National Guard. They lost men who enlisted in other units destined for active duty and remained under strength, although they were not officially disbanded until March 1919.

New Jersey also raised a state militia as a replacement for the Guardsmen called to active duty during World War I. A General Order of August 15, 1917, created a militia force of twenty-six infantry rifle companies and two machine gun companies, which were organized into six battalions, all composed of white recruits. In accordance with federal military segregation policy, the orders also authorized the raising of two "Separate Companies (colored)." One African American company was located in Atlantic City and the other in Newark. Most of the state militiamen were individuals not subject to federal conscription due to their age, minor disabilities or deferments due to dependents or essential war employment. The militia was disbanded in January 1920.

A third component of New Jersey's hodge-podge state force during the war was the State Militia Reserve, 106 small local units created by the legislature in 1918 to provide assistance to police forces and fire departments in guarding power plants and other public utilities. After the armistice was signed on November 11, 1918, attendance at militia reserve (and militia) drills decreased dramatically, and the organization faded away until it was formally disbanded at the same time as the militia in 1920.

The summer encampment held at Sea Girt in 1920 was the first training period for the revived New Jersey National Guard. The first unit of the new Guard was the Sixth New Jersey Infantry, recruited from interested and eligible members of the Fifth, Sixth and Seventh Battalions of the disbanded militia and commanded by former militia regimental commander Colonel Howard S. Borden, a socialite and polo player from Rumson. As in the prewar era, the encampment, with its drills and reviews, not only served as a training venue but also provided entertainment for visiting politicians and summer shore tourists. Borden's subsequent elevation to the rank of general, coupled with the desire of combat veteran officers, who considered him a feckless political appointee, to rejoin and reorganize the National Guard, initiated a feud that eventually had to be resolved by Governor Edward I. Edwards. Recruiting for lower ranks continued apace, however, with the Sea Girt annual training location serving as a big plus for attracting potential Guardsmen.

Potential recruits were told, "Uncle Sam offers you two weeks at the Seashore. All expenses paid. All equipment free." They were also advised, "Sea Girt offers ample opportunity for recreation and sport while the Guardsman is not on duty. There is swimming, boating and fishing, the site being in close proximity to many shore resorts." Despite the attractions, it was reported that "very few [WWI veterans] had any desire for further service in the National Guard at that time." Many of the new soldiers were men too young to have served in the war, including at least one underage fifteen-year-old whose father came to the camp to retrieve him.

Recruiting eventually picked up, and as more units were formed, Borden's 6th New Jersey faded away, replaced by World War I Twenty-ninth Division designations, including the 113th and 114th Infantry Regiments and 104th Engineer Regiment. By 1922, most of the new units were absorbed into the 44th Division, authorized by the National Defense Act of 1920. The 44th, which was formally recognized in March 1924, also included New York Guardsmen, and the colors of its blue and gold insignia patch were intended to recall the original Dutch heritage of New Netherland shared by both states. New support units, part of a modern divisional structure, were added throughout the 1920s and 1930s.

Governor A. Harry Moore reviewing New Jersey National Guard soldiers marching into Sea Girt for their annual training. *NGMMNJ.*

Soldiers of the 113th Infantry board a train in Newark train station in 1923 on their way to Sea Girt for annual training. *Joseph G. Bilby.*

New Jersey's only mounted unit, the old Essex Troop, or 1st New Jersey Cavalry Squadron, which had been divided between military police and artillery service in World War I, began to reorganize under veteran officers in 1920 and was redesignated the 102nd Cavalry on August 17, 1921. As part of the 51st Cavalry Brigade, the 102nd was not a component of the 44th Division but still came under the authority of New Jersey's adjutant general.

In 1928, New Jersey authorized its first National Guard Army Air Corps unit, the 119th Observation Squadron, although it took until January 30, 1930, for the squadron to achieve formal federal recognition and receive its first O-2H aircraft. The squadron, which took on the lineage of the World War I 119th Aero Squadron, established headquarters at the new Newark Airport, located in reclaimed saltwater meadowlands between Newark and Elizabeth. By 1932, the *Trenton Sunday Times-Advertiser* announced that Newark Airport was the busiest airport in the world, handling more than a quarter of the country's air traffic.

In a segregated military, the New Jersey National Guard remained a white-only organization. Although there were a few African American National Guard units in other states, the federal government would not authorize one for New Jersey. In response, African American citizens, as well as white and black World War I veterans, petitioned the state's adjutant general

The first plane assigned to the New Jersey National Guard's 119th Observation Squadron at Newark Airport in 1930. *NGMMNJ.*

and their state legislators to create a totally state-funded unit. In response, Assemblyman Frank S. Hargraves introduced such a bill, and on April 16, 1930, both houses of the New Jersey legislature passed Chapter 149, Laws of 1930, authorizing the "organization and equipment of a battalion of Negro infantry" at state expense. On July 14, 1931, committees were established to organize the first companies of what came to be called the First Separate Battalion, New Jersey State Militia. Companies were raised in Newark, Atlantic City and Camden. The battalion was later redesignated as the First Battalion, New Jersey State Guard.

World War II erupted in Europe in September 1939, and during the following year, America began to strengthen its military, including the National Guard. The New Jersey National Guard's strength in mid-1940, including nondivisional units like the 102nd Cavalry and 119th Observation Group, was 7,187 officers and men. In August 1940, the federal government called the 44th Division, along with most other National Guard units across the country, to active duty. The 44th, which also included New York's 71st

Sergeant Jackie Lombardo training soldiers of the 113th Infantry at the Sussex Avenue Armory in Newark at the time of the National Guard mobilization of September 1940. *Joseph G. Bilby.*

Infantry Regiment, was activated on September 16 and assigned to Fort Dix, where the 104th Engineers, as did their predecessor unit in World War I, designed and constructed a camp for the entire division as well as a reception center for draftees. The peacetime draft was enacted at the same time, and draftees and volunteer recruits from New Jersey and New York were soon assigned to bring the division up to full strength.

The 102nd Cavalry was called to active duty on January 6 and assigned to Fort Jackson, South Carolina, for training. The 102nd entered service as a horseback-mounted unit, and although the regiment gradually gave up its horses, one squadron remained mounted through April 1942. The 102nd would be the first New Jersey National Guard unit to go overseas.

With the approach of World War II, the 1st Separate Battalion was belatedly accepted by the federal government as a National Guard unit and redesignated as the First Battalion of the 372nd Infantry Regiment, composed of African American Guardsmen from the District of Columbia, Maryland, Massachusetts and Ohio. In World War I, the 372nd had established a distinguished combat record while detailed to the French army.

Most of the Guardsmen mobilized in 1940 had eagerly anticipated the end of their one year of federal service for training, and there was much

Soldiers of the 1st Separate Battalion after their mobilization as part of the 372nd Infantry Regiment in 1941. *NGMMNJ.*

New Jersey National Guard soldiers of the 44th Division's 114th Infantry stationed at Fort Dix in November 1940 were issued long underwear for the coming winter. *Joseph G. Bilby.*

grumbling when their service time was extended for another eighteen months by Congress in August 1941. In September, after spending nearly a year at Fort Dix, the Forty-fourth Division traveled to South Carolina to participate in the "Carolina Maneuvers," which lasted through early December. The men of the division were on their way back to Fort Dix when they heard the news of Pearl Harbor and realized that their active duty would last until the end of the war.

In February 1942, the 113th Infantry was detached from the division and assigned to the Eastern Defense Command. The regiment was strung out from Long Island to Delaware in company-sized posts intended to defend the coastline from saboteurs landed from submarines and never rejoined the 44th. The 113th subsequently moved around the country, serving as a local defense and training command until it was inactivated at Fort Rucker, Alabama, on September 25, 1945.

The 104th Engineer Regiment was also detached from the Division, with the first battalion sent to Camp Claiborne, Louisiana, as the 104th Engineer

Battalion and the second battalion transferred to Camp Pickett, Virginia, where it became the first battalion of the 175th Engineer Regiment. The 104th Battalion went on to Fort Lewis, Washington, and then the Pacific theater of war, from the Aleutian Islands to the Philippines, while the 175th participated in campaigns in North Africa and Italy.

The 44th Division, less the 113th, was transferred from Fort Dix to Camp Claiborne and then moved on to Fort Lewis, where it served as part of the United States' West Coast defenses throughout 1942. In early 1943, a number of men from the 71st and 114th Infantry, supplemented by draftees, were transferred to the 324th Infantry, a new regiment created within the division to replace the departed 113th. In early 1944, the 44th was shipped back to Louisiana for three months of field maneuvers and then on to Camp Phillips, Kansas, for final training before deployment overseas. When that task was accomplished, the division traveled by train to Camp Miles Standish in Massachusetts in August, its final stop before shipping out to Europe.

The Forty-fourth Division landed in Cherbourg, France, in mid-September 1944, trained intensively for a month and was then assigned to the Seventh Army. The Forty-fourth relieved the Seventieth Division in the front lines and was first engaged in combat on October 18, near Luneville, France, as part of an offensive to secure the passes through the Vosges Mountains. Less than a week after the offensive began, the division was struck by an intense German counterattack, which it defeated, inflicting heavy losses on the enemy.

In November, the Forty-fourth fought alongside the French Second Armored Division in a drive to liberate Strasbourg, broke through the Maginot Line on December 19 and then assumed a defensive position near Sarreguemines, where it defeated several German counterattacks. In late March 1945, the division relieved the Third Division, crossed the Rhine River at Worms and then advanced into Austria in early May, reaching Imst and Landeck as the war in Europe ended.

The 44th Division spent a short period of time on occupation duty in Austria and then returned to the United States in July 1945 for retraining prior to redeploying to the Pacific theater of war for the invasion of Japan. Fortunately, the Japanese surrendered before the 44th left the country again, and the division was deactivated that November. The 44th Division was in combat for 190 days and earned three Distinguished Unit Citations. Although its numerical designation was reassigned to an Illinois National Guard division in 1946, the lineage of the division's original New Jersey National Guard components, including the 113th and 114th Infantry Regiments, was transferred to new formations in the postwar New Jersey National Guard's 50th Armored Division.

The 119th Observation Squadron was called to active duty and detailed to coastal defense. Some members of the unit transferred to other units and served overseas. Perhaps the best known of these men was Donald Strait of Verona. Strait served as an enlisted man with the 119th but in early 1942 qualified as an aviation cadet and attended flight school at Maxwell Field, Alabama. Rising to the rank of captain, he became an ace, credited with 13.5 aerial victories over German aircraft as a fighter pilot in the 356th Fighter Group. After the war, Strait served in the New Jersey Air National Guard, from which he retired as a major general in 1978.

The former Separate Battalion officers and men, now part of the 372nd Infantry, were ordered into United States service on March 10, 1941. They were initially assigned to the Eastern Defense Command's First Army and stationed at Fort Dix as part of an internal defense force for the greater New York City area. Like the 113th, the 372nd later became a training unit and, in April 1944, a "rotational regiment," moving about the country to posts in Kentucky, Arizona and Washington, until arriving in Hawaii in April 1945 to prepare for the invasion of Japan. With the end of the war, the regiment returned to New Jersey and was inactivated at Fort Dix on January 31, 1946.

Around 560,500 New Jerseyans, including 10,000 women and 360,000 draftees, served in all branches of the armed forces during World War II. A total of 10,372 of them, including ten of the state's seventeen Medal of Honor awardees, made the ultimate sacrifice and were killed in action or died of wounds or other causes. Perhaps the most famous New Jersey soldier was USMC sergeant John Basilone of Raritan. Awarded the Medal of Honor for his actions in defense of Henderson Field on Guadalcanal in 1942, after a stint selling war bonds, Basilone requested a return to combat and was killed in action on Iwo Jima in February 1945.

For more detailed histories of the 102nd Cavalry and 1st Separate Battalion, see Bilby, Madden and Ziegler, Hidden History of New Jersey. *For an overview of New Jersey in World War II, see Lender,* One State in Arms.

CHAPTER 12

"THE FINEST THING
I HAVE SEEN"

THE IMMORTAL CHAPLAIN FROM NEWARK

S urvivor John Ladd remembered it as "the finest thing I have seen or hope to see this side of heaven." "It" became one of the iconic events of World War II, when four chaplains, two Protestant ministers, a Jewish rabbi and a Catholic priest, sacrificed their own lives on behalf of others as the torpedoed United States Army Transport (USAT) *Dorchester* slipped under the frigid North Atlantic waters in the early hours of February 3, 1943.

In the 1940s and 1950s, the story of the four heroic chaplains was one of the most well-known tragic tales of "the war," rivaling that of the five Sullivan brothers who went down aboard the USS *Juneau* off Guadalcanal on November 13, 1942. More than seven decades later, although some dedicated people preserve the memory, for the general public, the story of the chaplains has largely faded, along with the World War II generation itself, into the mist of history.

The *Dorchester* narrative resonated with particular strength in 1950s Newark, New Jersey, especially in the Catholic parish of Saint Rose of Lima in the Roseville section, where author Joseph Bilby attended the grammar school from which John Patrick Washington had graduated decades before. Washington, born the eldest son of an Irish immigrant family on July 18, 1908, was baptized, confirmed and served as an altar boy at Saint Rose and then went on to Seton Hall Preparatory School, Seton Hall College and Immaculate Conception Seminary, Darlington, where he was ordained a priest. His story, culminating in an episode of unparalleled heroism aboard the *Dorchester*, was a classic tale of Irish Catholic immigrant success and

A commemorative stamp was issued to honor the four chaplains in 1948. *Joseph G. Bilby.*

American patriotism writ large. The nuns of Saint Rose of Lima School never tired of repeating it to their students, and the parish priests would speak of it from the pulpit with regularity.

By all accounts, young John Washington was a good-humored lad who also manifested an early religious streak. In the sixth grade, he announced to his family that he wanted to become a priest. A near-death experience in high school, in which Washington ran a high fever so serious that he received Extreme Unction, the last rites of the Catholic Church, only to recover, while his sister died of the same ailment, seemed to solidify his idea, perhaps touched with a bit of survivor's guilt, that "God must have kept me here for something."

Although he occasionally expressed unhappiness with "pompous" clerics further up the hierarchy's chain of command, John Washington worked hard at Darlington Seminary, dedicated to fulfilling his dream of becoming a priest. He shook off minor annoyances and kept his eye on the ball, which he believed was "to help common people and win over their hearts" and was ordained in 1935.

Father Washington first served as a curate at Saint Genevieve's parish in Elizabeth and then at Saint Venantius in Orange and Saint Stephen's in Kearny, where he was named associate pastor. At Saint Stephen's, the young clergyman, a big Louis Armstrong fan as well as an amateur musician, played songs and bought records for the parish youth group, organized dances and established a choir. Father George Murphy, Saint Stephen's pastor, recalled that Washington quickly became his essential "right hand man" in administering the parish. Murphy assigned his popular assistant the complex job of organizing and promoting church social activities and overseeing the parish school, tasks the younger priest accepted with enthusiasm and a spirit that caused one parishioner to remember him as "a happy person." The personable Washington had begun what seemed an inevitable rise to the top in his chosen profession. And then came Pearl Harbor.

Father Washington was driving his widowed mother home from lunch and an afternoon movie when they heard the news of the Japanese attack on his car radio, and he immediately advised her of his desire to enlist. On his return to the rectory, Washington asked Father Murphy, a World War I veteran, for his permission and blessing to join the service. As he expected, Murphy acceded to his young colleague's wishes.

There was, however, a potential problem that had to be resolved before Father Washington could enlist. While a child in Newark, he had injured his right eye in a BB gun accident, which affected his eyesight and resulted in a need to wear glasses, which he feared would disqualify him from service. Although a poor swimmer, Washington initially applied to join the navy but was rejected, as he had feared, for failing to pass the eye test. Still determined to join the service, he applied to the army, where he followed Father Murphy's advice to cheat and cover his bad eye twice during the eye test. "They'll never notice," said Murphy. The pragmatic pastor was correct, and when John Washington followed his mentor's advice, albeit with a guilty conscience, he was accepted as an army chaplain and commissioned a first lieutenant.

Although uncomfortable with young men similar to those he had grown up with in his blue-collar Newark neighborhood saluting him, newly commissioned Chaplain Washington pinned on his silver bar and proceeded to Fort Benjamin Harrison, Indiana, for training in May 1942. After completing his chaplain branch officer basic school at the fort, he was assigned to the Seventy-sixth Infantry Division at Fort Meade, Maryland, from where he petitioned to be selected for overseas duty.

In November, Father Washington was ordered to Harvard University for an advanced chaplain's course, where he met the three other chaplains with whom he would gain fame: Reverend George L. Fox, a Methodist minister who had served in World War I as an enlisted man; Rabbi Alexander P. Goode, who counted Al Jolson among his relatives; and Reverend Clark

Left: Father John Washington. *St. Stephen's Parish, Kearny, NJ.*

Below: The USAT *Dorchester. NGMMNJ.*

V. Poling, son of a clergyman and a minister of the Reformed Church in America. In a display of wartime ecumenism, the men quickly became fast friends. After Harvard, all four were ordered to Camp Miles Standish, Massachusetts, where they received their overseas orders and were assigned to sail on the USAT *Dorchester* out of New York.

On January 23, 1943, the *Dorchester*, converted into a troop transport from a peacetime passenger liner designed to hold three hundred tourists, sailed from New York with more than nine hundred men, including the chaplains, aboard, headed for Greenland. Since German submarines prowled the seas, all the soldiers and crewmen were told to sleep in their clothes with life jackets nearby, but many men, confined to the deep, hot, hold of the ship, ignored the order.

At around 1:00 a.m. on February 3, the *Dorchester* was torpedoed amidships by a German submarine off the coast of Newfoundland and began to sink. Panicked soldiers, many still in their underwear and without life jackets, swarmed up to the deck, where Fox, Goode, Poling and Washington had already stationed themselves. The chaplains guided panic-stricken soldiers to a life jacket storage area and then, when those jackets were all handed out, gave up their own to those who had none.

The chaplains, calm and cool in the face of disaster, displayed outstanding leadership qualities, encouraging and assisting enlisted men to the few available lifeboats to get off the rapidly sinking *Dorchester*, which went down in twenty minutes. Numerous survivors recalled seeing the four men join hands and hearing them pray above the din in English, Latin and Hebrew as the ship finally slipped beneath the North Atlantic waves.

The 4 chaplains were among the 672 men who lost their lives aboard the *Dorchester*—230 survived. Although the ship was escorted by several Coast Guard vessels, the speed at which it sank provided little time to launch lifeboats, and sadly, many of the men the chaplains managed to get outfitted with life jackets died from exposure as they floated in thirty-four-degree water awaiting rescue.

When she heard the news that her beloved eldest son had died in the war, Mary Washington was devastated. The horror would not end for her there, though, as she suffered through multiple additional tragedies. She lost not only John but two of her other sons as well. Francis, an Army Air Corps bombardier, was killed in the Pacific, and Leo died of wounds incurred in the fighting in Europe. Mary Washington never left her Newark home after learning of John's death and died there several years later.

The memorial monument to Father Washington erected by St. Rose of Lima parish in Newark in 1960. *Joseph G. Bilby.*

Opposite, top: A number of New Jersey clergymen served as chaplains in World War II, including Father Aloysius S. Carney, here saying mass on a ration box altar in Italy. Carney became pastor of Saint Rose of Lima parish in Newark in 1958. *Steve Southwick.*

Opposite, bottom: In 1950, three World War II New Jersey veteran chaplains—(left to right) Catholic Father Aloysius S. Carney, Presbyterian Pastor David L. Coddington and Rabbi Gershon B. Chertoff—met to pay tribute to the four chaplains who went down with the *Dorchester*. *Steve Southwick.*

Although the story of the four chaplains has faded in the mind of the general public over the years since 1943, the memory of their heroism has been perpetuated by numerous monuments, including a modest one at Washington's Saint Rose parish in Newark, stained-glass windows, books and a documentary film, as well as a 1948 postage stamp, and

Dedication of the Four Chaplains Memorial monument at Saint Stephen's Church in Kearny. *Ed Civinskas.*

The memorial to the four chaplains at St. Stephen's Church in Kearny. *James M. Madden.*

there is a 501c-3 foundation in their name. In 1944, the chaplains were posthumously awarded the Purple Heart and Distinguished Service Cross, and in 1960, their next of kin received a special Congressional Medal of Valor in their honor. In 1988, Congress declared February 3 as "Four Chaplains Day."

The last of the 230 survivors of the *Dorchester* sinking, and thus the last living witness to the four chaplains' sacrifice, passed away on January 12, 2013. Three weeks later, Saint Stephen's parish, where John Washington spent his last days as a civilian, dedicated a memorial to him and his three comrades, ensuring that the public memory of their story, although it may flicker, will never truly die on "this side of heaven."

For more on the story of the four chaplains, see Kurzman, No Greater Glory.

CHAPTER 13

THE GREATEST NEW JERSEY WAR MYTH

For many years, historians, both academic and popular, repeated the story that New Jersey's shore town merchants, hell bent on not losing summer profits, sacrificed the greater good of the nation, and lives as well, and "refused to participate in blackout procedures," defying federal and state authorities by obstinately keeping the lights on at their boardwalk enterprises during World War II. The result of this, or so the story goes, was the silhouetting of passing merchant ships against a lit up skyline, making them easy targets for German submarines lurking offshore.

This oft-told tale of boardwalk perfidy and "reprehensible" behavior appears to have been originally spun by Pulitzer Prize–winning Harvard historian Samuel Eliot Morison. Morison, a scion of one of New England's elite families and a personal friend of President Franklin D. Roosevelt, was commissioned as an officer by the navy during World War II and assigned to write its wartime history. The result, *History of United States Naval Operations in World War II*, was published in fifteen volumes between 1947 and 1962. Morison was perhaps the best literary stylist among twentieth-century American historians, and one of the books in the series was awarded the coveted Bancroft Prize for historical writing.

Despite his seemingly impeccable credentials, it turns out that Morison erred, to be kind, in assigning blame to the Jersey Shore for the loss of merchant ships to German submarines. (He also held no one responsible for Pearl Harbor.) In his defense, Morison was probably fed the information by the navy as part of a campaign to excuse its poor performance in the initial stages of the U-boat

New Jersey governor Charles Edison, son of the inventor Thomas Edison. Edison served as governor from January 1941 to January 1944. *Joseph G. Bilby.*

war off the East Coast. An examination of the New Jersey governor's "War Cabinet Notes," recently made available online by the New Jersey State Archives, reveals a different, far more complex story.

The New Jersey War Cabinet, which was convened weekly during the conflict by Governor Charles Edison and his successor, Governor Walter Edge, had its origins in Governor A. Harry Moore's "Emergency Committee," which was created by Moore at the outbreak of the war in Europe in September 1939. The committee included the governor, the civilian defense director, the adjutant general, the state police superintendent and legislative leaders.

Soon after America's entry into the war in December 1941, five long-range German U-boats left their base in France and headed for the East Coast of the United States. British intelligence forwarded the information that the submarines were on their way west to the United States Navy, but to no avail. Rear Admiral Adolphus Andrews, commanding the American East Coast defense sector, did not have anywhere near the antisubmarine warfare vessels needed and apparently lacked the competence to effectively use what he did have available. Andrews refused to listen to British advice to group merchant ships in convoys that would be easier to escort and defend. When a U-boat sank a merchant ship off Long Island on January 14, 1942, Andrews failed to react in any significant way, and another vessel was torpedoed off Sandy Hook shortly afterward.

When the New Jersey War Cabinet first met on March 3, 1942, what the Germans officially dubbed "Operation Drum Beat" and unofficially called the "Happy Time," was well underway. Initial success had led the Germans to dispatch successive additional waves of U-boats to Canadian and United

States waters. Ships were torpedoed from Nova Scotia to Florida, including five in New Jersey waters between January and March.

As the crisis deepened, the British dispatched antisubmarine vessels with experienced crews to help protect the East Coast. Leonard Dreyfuss, an advertising executive who served as New Jersey's civilian defense director, advised Governor Edison that the army's Second Corps, supervising the defense of the New York–New Jersey area, had requested that "all lights along the New Jersey seacoast be dimmed or eliminated" for fear they would silhouette ships for targeting. Dreyfuss reported that municipal authorities in the shore communities had offered their full cooperation in the effort. The effort came late, since British intelligence had warned the navy as early as December that the U-boats were on their way, and the navy did nothing to prepare. The lights of New York City and various lightships and lighthouses seem to have been used by the Germans more for location and direction than silhouetting, however.

There may have been some silhouetting prior to the dim-out request being received and implemented, although even this scenario seems unlikely.

SS *R.P. Resor* sinking. *Joseph G. Bilby.*

The SS *R.P. Resor* was torpedoed eighteen miles off Lavallette on February 27, 1942. One of the two survivors recalled that he could see the lights of Manasquan at some unspecified time prior to the ship's being hit, although it should be noted that the *Resor* was sunk in February, not the tourist season, and at around midnight, when the vast majority of New Jersey coastal residents were in bed. The *Resor*'s vulnerability was most likely exacerbated by the fact that the night was "brilliantly lit" by a full moon. Captain Gardner F. Clark of the SS *Lemuel Burrows* claimed he could see the lights of Atlantic City as he passed close to shore on the night of March 13–14, 1942. It was not the tourist season, and although Atlantic City would have been well lit in the evening simply because it was a city as well as a resort, the *Burrows* was torpedoed at 8:00 a.m. on March 14, which, by anyone's definition, was broad daylight.

Unfortunately, throughout the rest of the year, the army and the navy were ambivalent, unclear and often contradictory as to which lighting—boardwalk, inland business, street and home or automotive—they wanted "dimmed or eliminated." The navy apparently declined to follow its own suggestions, keeping "3,000 to 5,000 exterior lights" lit all night on the seaward side of its Cape May installation. Ironically, after observing the coast from the sea in March, the navy expressed itself "quite satisfied with the results of the dim-out between Atlantic Highlands and Sea Girt, that the dim-out between Sea Girt and Atlantic City was fair, but not good between Atlantic City and Cape May." In April, Director Dreyfuss personally inspected Asbury Park and found that "the town was in almost total darkness."

Conflicting reports continued to come in. Navy officials reported being able to see lights from Atlantic City and Cape May out at sea but also declared that the results of another offshore survey were "satisfactory." In mid-May, the navy took Dreyfuss out for a look-see, and the director reported that the dim-out was "about as perfect as could be expected." The army, on the other hand, now wanted the dim-out extended as much as fifteen miles inland, with all exterior lighted signage and streetlights shut down. It should be noted that ships sunk by German submarines were torpedoed an average of twelve miles off the coast—and that many, at least initially, were sailing fully lighted themselves.

Despite occasional complaints, a June 1, 1942 survey of the shore from New York to Long Branch by state authorities revealed that "the lighting in New Jersey did not in any way reflect a glare on the waters which would silhouette a ship." Although the army's Second Corps command agreed, the navy maintained again that the dim-out was "not sufficient" at Wildwood Crest and Atlantic City. In return, the state noted that, as before, the naval station at Cape May provided the exception to an otherwise satisfactory situation, as its lights could be seen far out at sea. A dredge working at the base was described as being "lit up like a Christmas tree."

Despite dramatic reductions in coastal lighting, vessels continued to be sunk, as the navy struggled to develop an efficient antisubmarine campaign, a lack of which was the true cause of the shipping losses. In June, a seven-mile stretch of beach south of Asbury Park, from Belmar to Manasquan, was covered with "oil and tar residue" and debris from torpedoed ships, requiring the state to request WPA workers to clean up the mess. One Spring Lake resident at the time recalls retrieving a .45-caliber automatic pistol from a beached and abandoned lifeboat.

In July, the navy, still casting about to blame someone else for its own deficiencies, and despite the fact that it had recently declared that it was "quite satisfied" with the absence of coastal lighting, complained to the state that lights at Asbury Park were silhouetting ships at sea. In response, Director Dreyfuss and state police superintendent Colonel Charles H. Schoeffel, a World War I veteran, personally visited Asbury Park on two separate occasions. Drefyuss rated the city's effort as a "splendid job," while Schoeffel reported that the dim-out was "quite effective."

New Jersey State Police superintendent colonel Charles H. Schoeffel was a major participant in the governor's war cabinet discussions. The ribbons on Schoeffel's chest were earned during his army service in World War I. *New Jersey State Police Archives.*

In addition to shoreline dim-outs, "blackouts" were conducted in various inland regions of the state as part of a defense against potential air attacks. They were taken seriously, unlikely as that might seem in retrospect, considering

"Blackout drills" were held in Newark prior to and after the beginning of World War II. This is a view of Newark, looking down Broad Street just prior to a prewar blackout. *Joseph G. Bilby.*

the aircraft technology available to the Germans at the time. Strange as it may seem now, army officers told state officials that when German civilians realized they were being bombed by American planes, the Luftwaffe would surely have to bomb America in return to keep morale up. The governor certainly believed in the possibility and installed a bombproof vault to protect his famous father's papers at the Edison West Orange laboratory.

What the dim-outs and blackouts did produce, according to New Jersey officials and Mayor Fiorello LaGuardia of New York City, was an increase in vehicle accidents and a spike in crime. Automobiles were restricted to using parking lights only (later on headlights were allowed to be partially masked) while night driving in coastal dim-out areas. A survey revealed that in Cape May County, where there had been no fatal automobile accidents in 1941, eleven people died in car crashes between January and October 1942. Director Dreyfuss reported a similar increase in New York and noted that London had experienced a 100 percent increase in automotive fatalities under blackout conditions. Interestingly, most of the traffic summonses issued to motorists for violating the car headlight policy in Cape May were to navy officers.

While army, navy and state authorities continued to wrangle over the total effectiveness of the coastal dim-out, no one ever argued that it was not being implemented or that shore town businessmen were deliberately disregarding the policy, directly busting the longstanding myth propagated by Morison. By July 1942, antisubmarine warfare tactics began to take effect and by September, the Germans recognized that the "Happy Time" had ended. Although submarines remained a danger, the number of ship sinkings declined steadily from then to the end of the war. Unfortunately, the canard against New Jersey's boardwalk merchants survived far longer.

For further reading, see Gannon, Operation Drumbeat; *Gentile,* Shipwrecks of New Jersey; *and the New Jersey Governor's War Cabinet notes online at http://www. nj.gov/state/archives/szwaa001.html.*

CHAPTER 14

A JERSEY GIRL GOES TO WAR

The text on the back of the original photo, dated "6/11/42,"
read: "AMERICAN GIRL PILOT SERVES BRITISH FERRY
SERVICE, LONDON: American pilots, men and women, now serve with
Britain's Air Transport Auxiliary. Women number one to every ten men
in the service. Here Virginia Farr, a New Jersey lass, adjusts her parachute
preparatory to a flight."

So who was Virginia Farr, where in New Jersey was she from and what
exactly was she doing in Britain in 1942? That would take a bit of research,
and the story that unfolded would shed some light on a little-known group
of American women who served abroad during World War II.

According to the 1940 U.S. census, Virginia Farr was born in 1919 in
Massachusetts and resided in Rochester, New York, in 1935. In 1940, the
twenty-one-year-old Farr was living at 572 Prospect Avenue in West Orange,
New Jersey, in the home of her seventy-eight-old grandmother, Maria H.
Farr, along with her father, Barclay H. Farr, age forty-nine; her mother,
Evelyn G. Farr, forty-four; and her eighteen-year-old brother Peter R. Farr.
The family was apparently quite well to do and had a live-in cook, as well
as a housekeeper. The Farrs' chauffer and his wife and son also lived at the
West Orange address.

Barclay Farr listed his occupation as "executor and guardian," and his wife
claimed she was an interior decorator who owned her own business. Mr. Farr
stated that his income for the previous year was $5,000, a fair piece of change
in 1940, but Mrs. Farr reported that she had had no earnings from her business.

ATA pilot Virginia Farr of West Orange adjusts her parachute before taking off in a Spitfire in Britain in June 1942. *Joseph G. Bilby.*

A search in the *New York Times* revealed that the Farr family had been wealthy for some time. Virginia's grandfather and Barclay's father, Philadelphia-born Thomas H.P. Farr, had died in 1938. His obituary noted that he had attended private school in Switzerland and then Princeton University, where he played football, made Phi Beta Kappa and graduated in the class of 1881. Farr subsequently worked for several Wall Street firms (one of which he was a partner in), was the founder and president of the First National Bank of West Orange and also had financial interests in Peru.

He was a founding member of the Essex County Country Club, located across the street from his home, and a well-known polo player.

So how did Thomas Farr's granddaughter end up in England wearing a parachute? Some further research led to the British Air Transport Auxiliary (ATA) website, which revealed that Virginia was one of twenty-five female pilots recruited in early 1942 for the ATA by Jacqueline "Jackie" Cochrane, president of the "Ninety-Nines," a female pilots' organization founded by Amelia Earhart. Cochrane enlisted the best pilots she could find for the British expedition. Farr, then twenty-four, had over one thousand hours of flying time and was a certified instructor and active member of the organization, so she was a natural choice.

Farr and the other women traveled to Great Britain via Canada by ship through submarine-infested waters in March 1942. She and her compatriots, who became the only American female pilots in the ATA, went through a brief training period and then began to ferry Spitfire and Hurricane fighter planes from factories to RAF bases around the British Isles, a year before female ferry pilots were recruited for United States service. A *New York Times* article published on June 1, 1942, quoted Farr, the only Jersey Girl in the group, as saying she was "having the time of my life and would not have missed it for anything." Eventually, the ATA women ferried all types of aircraft, including bombers and, in the final months of the war, expanded their operations to the European continent.

Virginia Farr served in the ATA through June 1945. At the end of the war, she "returned to the United States with her English friend and partner, Vivian Jeffery." They moved to California, where they established the V-2 ranch and raised Hereford cattle and Corgi dogs. Farr, a pioneer woman in military flight, passed away in 1988. She left behind a long-overlooked tale well worth telling. Hopefully this essay will begin to redress that omission.

For further reading on the American women in the ATA, see: http://www.airtransportaux.com.

CHAPTER 15

THE WAR AT HOME

In 1941, most Americans wanted nothing to do with another world war, but it arrived, uninvited, at their doorstop with the bombing of Pearl Harbor on December 7. In New Jersey, many families were listening to the Giants football game on radio station WHN when an urgent news bulletin announcing the attack interrupted the broadcast. Across the state, frantic listeners rushed to their telephones to commiserate with loved ones, while thousands of men mobbed recruiting stations the next morning. The war was on, and it would profoundly change New Jersey—and the country—on a multitude of levels.

In those dark early days of war, public anxiety ran high over perceived threats both at home and abroad. On the local front, the German-American Bund, a virulent pro-Nazi organization, had raised the ire of the American Legion, Jewish war veterans and numerous other groups prior to the outbreak of the war. The Bund, headquartered in New York City, maintained a summer camp and resort, Camp Nordland, near Andover in Sussex County. In the 1930s, Nordland was the site of ceremonies and rallies celebrating a bizarre Nazi fantasyland. The camp was dominated by a large recreation hall featuring a prominent portrait of Hitler on an inside wall. On Memorial Day 1941, the Sussex county sheriff raided Nordland, arrested Bund leader Gerhard Kunze and closed the camp down. Kunze was later released, but when accused of counseling men to avoid the military draft, he fled to Mexico.

Although it seems unlikely in retrospect, after Pearl Harbor (Germany and Italy declared war on the United States in the immediate aftermath), New

Jerseyans feared Axis attacks on the state from the sea and air. A December 1941 Gallup poll indicated that 45 percent of East Coast residents were convinced that enemy attacks would hit their cities. At least in the early days of the conflict, government officials were seriously troubled by the possibility as well. In early 1942, New Jersey governor Charles Edison's War Cabinet members requested the identification and location of an estimated ten thousand telephone and power company personnel in preparation for a response to possible air raids. Governor Edison ordered guards stationed at a large gasoline storage tank adjacent to several factories in Harrison, because a tank explosion "would undoubtedly destroy most of the plants in the vicinity." Rumors of a possible attack were rampant, and War Cabinet members mulled over the news of a new type of German bomb, described as "a very destructive combination incendiary and explosive bomb which is difficult to control." A March 1943 radio announcement by Reichsmarschall Hermann Goering, commander of the German Luftwaffe and a notorious windbag, boasting that Americans could expect New York, Washington and Boston to be bombed, only heightened concerns. In response, state officials conducted and analyzed the effectiveness of air raid drills and blackouts, which had actually been initiated in the prewar period, and were particularly displeased when some did not run according to plan. A November 1942 drill in Trenton, for example, created "considerable confusion" among employees at the statehouse, while a city police officer allowed cars to proceed "at a rapid rate of speed" during the exercise.

Certainly, some of the War Cabinet's fears were not unfounded, considering a string of deadly German U-boat attacks from mid-January to mid-June 1942 that included several ships torpedoed off the New Jersey coast. On January 25, 1942, German submarine U-130 torpedoed the Norwegian tanker *Varanger*, twenty-eight nautical miles off the coast. The explosion shook windows in Sea Isle City and could be heard in Atlantic City. Other ships lost off the shore included the tanker *R.P. Resor*, its flames visible from Manasquan after a February 1942 attack. The following month, shore residents along Barnegat Bay saw the tanker *Gulftrade* explode in flames. Despite dramatic reductions in coastal lighting, vessels continued to be sunk as American army and navy leaders scrambled to build an effective antisubmarine defense and convoy system. The turning point came in mid-April, when a German submarine was destroyed by exploding depth charges from a U.S. warship off North Carolina. More kills followed, and by the end of summer, the submarine threat was greatly reduced.

STATE OF NEW JERSEY

OFFICIAL AIR RAID SIGNALS

From the time you FIRST HEAR SIRENS
KEEP LIGHTS OUT until you hear ALL CLEAR

A LONG STEADY BLAST IS THE **BLUE SIGNAL**	DO THIS	Turn OFF LIGHTS in Homes, Stores, Offices
		Pedestrians and Traffic may continue to move
MEANS PLANES APPROACHING		Street Lights Remain On
		Turn Radio On
		Don't Use Phone

A FLUCTUATING OR INTERMITTENT BLAST IS THE **RED SIGNAL**	DO THIS	ALL LIGHTS OUT
		All Traffic Stops
MEANS PLANES OVERHEAD		Stay Inside—If Outside, Seek Shelter
		Turn Off Gas Burners—But not Pilot Light
		Keep Radio On
		Don't Use Phone

A LONG STEADY BLAST (ALWAYS FOLLOWS RED) IS THE **BLUE SIGNAL**	DO THIS	DON'T Turn On Lights even tho Street Lights Go On
		Pedestrians and Traffic May Proceed with Caution
MEANS PLANES MAY RETURN		Keep Radio On (You'll need it for All Clear)
		Don't use Phone

ALL CLEAR WILL BE ANNOUNCED TO HOUSEHOLDERS BY **RADIO**	DO THIS	Turn On Lights — Blackout Ended
		A single short blast will notify Protective Forces of ALL CLEAR

WHAT TO DO IN THE EVENT OF A GAS ATTACK

1. KEEP CALM—A gas bomb will not poison a whole city block—you can always escape.

2. ALL bursting bombs SMELL, whether they contain war gas or not. Get away from the odor.

3. If INDOORS, stay there. Go upstairs. Close doors, windows, stuff wet towels into large cracks.

4. If OUTDOORS, hold your breath as long as possible. Get out of danger zone. HOLD A WET HANDKERCHIEF TO YOUR MOUTH.
   There are two kinds of gas.

5. CHOKING GAS is GONE in 15 minutes. Do not rub eyes. If throat burns, wash with water. LIE ABSOLUTELY STILL UNTIL DOCTOR ARRIVES. Quiet drives gas from lungs. NO STIMULANTS.

6. The other is BLISTER GAS. It lasts longer. STINGS skin, nose, eyes. Get away from it. TIME IS IMPORTANT. Remove affected clothing and place outside. WITHIN FIVE MINUTES lather skin and hair with old-fashioned yellow laundry soap, rinse with lots of water. RUN WATER ON EYES. TIME IS IMPORTANT: IMMEDIATE SELF-AID with water prevents blisters. WASH AT ONCE. Then call doctor. DO NOT BREAK BLISTERS.

Your Air Raid Wardens Are

Name Mr. Wentworth   Street 15 Newfield Street

Name Mr. Atkinson   Street 33 Newfield Street

Your Block Leader Is

Name Katherine Elberty   Street 19 Newfield Street

CONSULT YOUR BLOCK LEADER FOR INFORMATION ON—VICTORY GARDENS—NUTRITION—CANNING—HEALTH AND WELFARE—CHILD CARE—CONSUMER INFORMATION—RECREATION, SALVAGE AND OTHER WAR ACTIVITIES

 By order of Governor Charles Edison this card is to be placed on the kitchen wall nearest the dining room or living room door for the duration. Must also be displayed prominently in stores, offices and public places.

C   97500

 Leonard Dreyfuss
Civilian Defense Director.

SCOTT PRINTING CO. JERSEY CITY, N. J.

A poster advising residents of East Orange on what to do during an air raid.

As New Jersey worked its way through the traumatic early days of war, the state's industrial base shifted into high gear, producing everything from battleships and aircraft carriers to the B-25 bomber engines that powered Lieutenant Colonel James "Jimmy" Doolittle's raiders over Tokyo in 1942. State businesses received more than $12 billion worth of defense contracts

Camden-based RCA Victor promoted war bond sales in its advertising. *Joseph G. Bilby.*

and New Jersey's industrial workforce doubled to more than one million workers. Enormous contributions to the war effort flowed from factories throughout the state. The New York Shipbuilding Company built twenty-nine capital ships in Camden for the navy. The Curtiss-Wright Corporation of Paterson produced more than 139,000 airplane engines. In Trenton, the Switlik Parachute Company's productivity was so impressive that the War Department presented it with the first of five army-navy "E" awards in 1942. One of Switlik's contributions was five hundred para-dummies—fireworks-armed rubber decoys, attached to parachutes and dropped behind enemy lines during the Allied D-day invasion in 1944. The decoys, which exploded with a sound similar to gunfire when they made contact with the ground, were intended to distract German troops from the actual drop zones where live paratroopers were landing.

Such a staggering output demanded a large workforce, and the need for workers fueled both opportunities and hardships, particularly for African Americans. Federal directives made racial discrimination illegal in hiring for war-contract jobs, and thousands of black New Jerseyans found employment that had been unavailable to them in New Jersey factories in the prewar era. African American jobseekers moved to the state from the south as well, and southern New Jersey saw an influx of Bahamian and Jamaican workers who immigrated with federal assistance to fill an agricultural labor shortage.

The rapid assimilation of African Americans into a traditionally white workforce was reflective of a national trend and led to racial antagonism and discrimination both on and off the job. As Colonel Charles H. Schoeffel, superintendent of state police, reported to the War Cabinet after attending a Detroit conference on race relations in 1943, the issue was one of national concern. Race riots had occurred in California, Texas, New York, Michigan and at a number of military bases that summer. The most disturbing confrontation took place in Detroit, where an altercation between black and white youths on a warm evening in June escalated into a citywide riot that resulted in the deaths of thirty-four people, twenty-five of them African Americans.

In New Jersey, the racial confrontations were smaller in scope but still deeply disturbing. Often, the bitter exchanges were between white soldiers, many from other states, often from the South, and black civilians. Police narrowly averted such a clash at a Passaic saloon in June 1943 but were forced to seek the help of military policemen stationed at the Paterson Armory when a crowd of angry black civilians gathered near Main Avenue later that evening. The arrival of the troops fortunately defused the situation. In the small rural community of Bordentown, frequent altercations resulted when

As an industrial state, New Jersey played an important part in the war effort. Here, Jersey girls rivet an Avenger torpedo bomber together at the General Motors Eastern Aircraft Division in Ewing Township, outside Trenton, in 1943. In all, the factory turned out 7,546 Avengers during the war. *Joseph G. Bilby.*

soldiers from nearby Fort Dix congregated in taverns and neighborhoods traditionally frequented by local African Americans.

Women, too, faced opportunities and challenges as they were absorbed into the massive workforce New Jersey needed to fuel the war machine. They joined the ranks of employees on assembly lines and in manufacturing and even management jobs, filling the void left by departing husbands, brothers, sons and boyfriends. By the end of 1942, 76 percent of Bell Telephone employees were women. "Rosie the Riveter" Jersey girls filled factories, and by 1943, most of the production workers on the Avenger torpedo bomber assembly line at the General Motors Eastern Aircraft Division in Ewing Township were women.

For many female defense workers, the prospect of a decent salary was dampened by overt hostility expressed by men who didn't believe women belonged in heavy industry. Elizabeth Hawes, a journalist who worked in

Women were a big part of the national and New Jersey war effort. Mrs. Marie Conroy of South Eighteenth Avenue in Newark was a mother of six, the oldest serving in the army, when this photo was taken of her working for a shipbuilding company in 1942. *Joseph G. Bilby.*

the gear department at the Wright Aeronautical Plant in Paterson with the intention of writing a book about her experience, recounted the resentment of her male co-workers. Their popular lament, she wrote, was: "Women, women, women: What's going to happen after the war? Will the men ever get their jobs back?" In addition to negative male attitudes, Hawes and many of her female co-workers on the third shift (midnight to 8:00 a.m.) also endured an exhausting regimen of domestic chores by day before reporting to work at night. Hawes, married with a five-year-old son, recalled her grueling schedule: "You come home about 8:30 a.m., eat some breakfast or dinner or whatever you call it. Then you know you'd better get to bed quick because if you want to get your child from school or want to have dinner with your husband…you must be up around 5:00 p.m."

Despite difficulties, however, women found factory war work empowering and meaningful and bonded over conversations that captured the pressing issues in their hectic lives. These topics of discussion, according to Hawes, included "the price of food; the sleep or the no sleep; the sick children or husbands; the hours it took to get to work…" As she reflected on the significance of her war work, Elizabeth Hawes pondered, "Can people be heroic without knowing it?"

While the home fires burned brightly, thousands of New Jersey's men and women headed off to fight the Axis enemies. A number of them in the Army Air Corps passed through basic training in Atlantic City, dubbed "Camp Boardwalk," where the government leased a number of hotels to house trainees and also provide, later in the war, rest and recreation for returning airmen. More than 560,000 state residents served in the armed forces, about 360,000 as draftees. An estimated 10,000 New Jersey women enlisted in the armed forces women's auxiliary forces, including the navy WAVES and army WAAC.

New Jersey African American soldiers and sailors also contributed to the war effort, although they were required to serve in all-black outfits since the American military was still legally segregated. The separation reflected a broader level of racial discrimination that permeated all levels of society throughout the country, albeit more dramatically in the southern states. In response to racial inequality, the nation's largest black organization, the National Association for the Advancement of Colored People (NAACP), advocated a "Double V" campaign that sought to secure victory against the Axis overseas and against segregation at home. NAACP pressure on the Roosevelt administration resulted in the Marine Corps acceptance of African Americans in its ranks for the first time in its history, albeit in a segregated unit. The organization's lobbying also pushed the navy to commission its first group of black officers and led to the eventual desegregation of officer training in all branches of the armed forces.

On the homefront, civilians pined for their loved ones at war, and reams of correspondence detailed the disruption, loneliness and frustration caused by the global conflict. Marian Merritt, a night duty nurse whose husband, an enlisted man in the 163rd Signal Photo Company, went overseas in August 1943, conveyed her sorrow and longing in one of many letters: "When I stop and think of how completely happy we could be, darling, it just about breaks my heart. To realize that this awful thing will go on indefinitely, that I can't even begin to plan for our future together." Happily, Merritt returned safely; many did not.

Maintaining the morale of the fighting men and women at an all-time high was a homefront priority, and New Jersey did its share to entertain and motivate the troops. Women and girls were reminded to stay positive and provide inspiration for the men overseas, and lonely GIs collected modest "pin-up" photos of pretty ingénues like Judy Garland and Betty Grable, who represented the wholesome girls waiting for them at home. The USO, or United Service Organization, played a pivotal role in raising troops' morale. The group provided social clubs at military bases, where enthusiastic soldiers could mingle with young female volunteers. At New Jersey's Camp Kilmer, the USO hostesses were affectionately known as "Kilmer Sweethearts," and volunteer Eleanore DeFelipo recalled with affection the ardent appreciation she received from the grateful GIs. "You felt like the belle of the ball. One soldier after another would cut in to dance with you!" she recalled.

The excitement of wartime, however, was more than matched by drudgery and deprivation. Material scarcity on the civilian market was a bleak reality. New automobile tires became unavailable in early 1942, followed by

Dear Friend: Don't look now—but as we "make with the arms" that's supposed to be a "V" (for Victory) we're forming! Those are bonds we're holding, so take a hint—and buy more—and more Cordially, Frank Sinatra Paul Brenner

Hoboken's Frank Sinatra joined WAAT radio host Paul Brenner of "Requestfully Yours" in selling war bonds in Newark in 1943. *Joseph G. Bilby.*

Film star Fifi D'Orsay entertained the soldiers of the 113th Infantry, New Jersey National Guard, at Fort Dix in 1941. *Joseph G. Bilby.*

rationing restrictions on gas, fuel oil, sugar, meat and butter. Shortages of fuel oil and coal weighed particularly on the minds of state officials as bitter winter months approached. Aggravating the situation, according to the governor's War Cabinet members, was the fact that essential personnel, such as coal dealers and their employees, were being drafted. "For example, the owner of a coal company with ten trucks received notice from the draft board for induction," Cabinet minutes noted on September 25, 1943. "This means his concern will be dissolved and 10 trucks taken out of service. This man is just as important to the war effort as a coal dealer as he would be a soldier."

Despite the grinding limitations of rationing, however, civilians found innovative ways to cope. Americans were urged by the secretary of agriculture to "dig for victory," turning their backyards and vacant lots into victory gardens. These unassuming plots of land eventually yielded about 40 percent of all vegetables consumed domestically during the war. A rite of each wartime spring was the trip to the crowded store counter to vie for the scarce seeds that could produce a multitude of meals. There were some rather unexpected innovations as well. In 1942, Newark's Dugan Brothers Bakery tried out wooden tires on its delivery trucks.

As civilians struggled with the demands, hopes and disappointments of daily life, another drama was quietly playing itself out on the domestic scene. Scattered throughout the state were closely guarded POW camps

A "Victory Garden" producing symbolic tanks and aircraft as portrayed by New Jersey Bell Telephone Company in a 1942 newsletter. *Joseph G. Bilby.*

that housed captured German and Italian soldiers, shipped to this country because the number of prisoners being held in Great Britain, close to the actual combat zone, was considered at capacity. From 1942 through 1945, more than 400,000 Axis prisoners were shipped to the United States and detained in camps across the country. In New Jersey, POW camps included sites at Belle Mead, Fort Dix, Jersey City Quartermaster Supply Depot,

German prisoners of war at Fort Dix put on a play, *Froh Und Heiter,* for their fellow POWs in April 1944. *Joseph G. Bilby.*

Camp Kilmer, Fort Monmouth, Raritan Arsenal, Metuchen and the Somerville Quartermaster Supply Depot.

Due to the homefront labor shortage, many POWs were put to work at canneries, mills, farms and other businesses and transferred to small temporary camps close to their assigned work areas. The Parvin State Park camp housed an estimated 150 POWs who labored in three separate shifts at nearby Seabrook Farms. Like many such camps, the Parvin facility was situated in an isolated area of the state. It was enclosed by a single wire fence ten feet high, with guard towers at each corner of the square enclosure, which was illuminated at night by floodlights.

Given that the prisoners were well fed and treated humanely, few attempted to escape; the army recorded a little more than two thousand attempts, less than 1 percent of the total number of POWs. Germans held at Fort Dix were comfortable enough to make costumes and put on a play for their fellow prisoners. Hans Bergmann, a detainee at Parvin, was one of the few, mostly dedicated Nazis, who did attempt escape. Bergmann, captured in the surrender of the Afrika Korps, was working at a Vineland cannery when he managed to elude his guards. He later told authorities he decided to flee the camp after receiving a letter from his mother, who wrote that an old family friend in Philadelphia would take care of him. Apparently unsuccessful in

How American it is . . . to want something better!

SURE this war-plant worker looks forward to "something better"—resuming study for her chosen career, that long-planned trip or to marriage.

That's why she's putting a healthy part of her earnings into war bonds and stamps—to speed the return of peace and all the other things which help make this "the land of something better."

Some of us can help most in the front lines, others on production lines —*all* of us can buy war bonds and stamps!

EVEN IN WARTIME, free America still enjoys many "better things" which are not available to less fortunate peoples. P. Ballantine & Sons, makers of "something better" in moderate beverages—Ballantine—America's largest selling ale.

P. Ballantine & Sons, Newark, N. J.

In 1943, Newark's Ballantine brewery encouraged female war workers to buy war bonds with this magazine advertisement. *Joseph G. Bilby.*

his efforts to find the family friend, an unshaven Bergmann turned himself into Philadelphia police and was placed in solitary confinement at Parvin. Two weeks later, the distraught prisoner killed himself by using a razor to slash his wrist and throat. Cooperative Italian prisoners were given a good deal of freedom following Italy's surrender in September 1943, and by late 1944, it was clear to all but the most hardened Nazis among the German POWs that the course of the war had clearly shifted in the Allies' favor and that it was best to cooperate with their captors.

For New Jersey's civilians, life began to seem more promising and hopeful by the end of 1944. Germany surrendered unconditionally on May 7, 1945, and Japan was clearly on the ropes. As the fighting in Europe and Asia began winding down, New Jersey shore vacationer Bertha Cole chronicled a flurry of victories in her diary, next to notations about mundane domestic events. On August 10, Cole wrote, "Tokyo broadcast its surrender acceptance!" followed by a comment about the local PTA sale. In a large, conspicuously scripted August 14 entry, she scrawled "Peace has come to the world today!" in reference to Japan's surrender, which effectively ended World War II. Farther down the page, she wrote, "Girls forbidden to swim [in a friend's pool] for fear of polio."

Perhaps it was fitting that Cole juxtaposed some of the momentous events of World War II with the rigors and routines of daily life. Like countless others struggling on the New Jersey homefront and throughout the country, her experience during those dark war years had been a strange mix of life-altering global events and the mundane everyday grind of getting by. As the storm clouds of war began to dissipate, Cole and millions of other civilians faced a dramatically altered new world that would result in enormous changes at home and abroad. The war was over, but the challenges had just begun.

For further reading, see Lender, One State in Arms *and Lurie and Veit,* New Jersey: A History.

CHAPTER 16

SENATOR McCARTHY PAYS A VISIT TO NEW JERSEY

B y the late 1940s, evil had taken on a new and frighteningly vivid persona for the American public. While Nazism and fascism, embodied by the Axis forces during World War II, had represented the epitome of danger less than a decade before, the newest threat to American security was the ever-expanding influence of Communism, promoted by a recent wartime ally— the Soviet Union. The growing power of the Soviets and the "iron curtain" they dropped across Eastern Europe represented an enormous threat to the global status quo, and the United States government feared that the rest of Europe might soon fall to the Red Menace.

In 1946, Americans became aware of espionage efforts in North America when a disgruntled agent at the Soviet embassy in Toronto defected and produced documents identifying spies working in the United States and Canada. A subsequent investigation eventually led to the arrest of Julius and Ethel Rosenberg, who became central figures in the nation's anticommunist debate, as they were apprehended in the fall of 1949, just after the Soviets exploded their first atomic bomb. Popular sentiment decreed that the Soviet Union could not have developed the bomb without help from spies in the West, and Julius Rosenberg had indeed relayed details on the bomb provided by Ethel's brother, David Greenglass, to the Soviets, although the degree of Ethel's actual involvement remains in dispute. Their conviction and subsequent execution in 1953 solidified that opinion.

Apprehension resulting from actual espionage contributed to a national sense of fear and paranoia, providing a perfect political opportunity to exploit by demagogues like Senator Joseph McCarthy of Wisconsin, a shrewd, yet insecure and defensive man who was desperately searching for a way to revitalize his flagging political career in 1950. The solution to his problem became apparent to him when he received favorable publicity for accusing a Wisconsin newspaper and its editor of "Communist leanings." Grafting a vital sense of urgency onto existing fears, McCarthy embarked on a four-year witch hunt that fueled public hysteria and disrupted countless lives. His vindictive campaign eventually included allegations of a spy ring at Fort Monmouth, Eatontown, and Camp Evans, Wall Township, two New Jersey installations that played vital roles in military research. McCarthy's relentless investigations would impact the lives of numerous government workers at the two bases.

Born on a Wisconsin farm and raised a devout Catholic, McCarthy graduated from Marquette University and pursued a less than stellar career as a lawyer, playing poker to supplement his income. Initially a staunch supporter of President Roosevelt and the New Deal, a disgruntled McCarthy switched his allegiance to the Republican Party after failing to secure the Democratic nomination for district attorney. During World War II, McCarthy joined the U.S. Marines, where he served as an intelligence officer for an air squadron and with typical bluster would later claim he flew thirty-two missions against the Japanese in the Pacific. In truth, he held a desk job but did fly on a few missions, most, if not all, of which were training exercises, to pad his résumé for postwar political purposes.

Following the war, McCarthy successfully ran as a Republican for a Wisconsin United States Senate seat, but his first years in office were marred by an unimpressive legislative performance and nagging allegations of tax offenses and bribery. Concerned that he would not retain his seat in the next election, McCarthy met with his closest advisors for advice on how to resuscitate his ailing career. He was particularly impressed with the suggestion from Edmund Walsh, a Roman Catholic priest who proposed that the senator build on his budding anticommunist reputation and initiate a campaign against "Communist subversives" within the Democratic administration of President Harry S. Truman.

An inspired McCarthy enlisted the help of close friend Jack Anderson, a Washington beltway columnist and investigative reporter who provided the senator with the names of politicians and government employees who were suspected of being communists.

McCarthy began his full-scale anticommunist crusade by alleging, in a talk before the Republican Women's Club of Wheeling, West Virginia, in

February 1950, that the State Department was riddled with communist agents. Following his reelection in 1952, he vigorously continued his campaign. In the fall of 1953, the army issued a release revealing that several employees at the Fort Monmouth radar laboratory had been suspended for security violations. The investigation leading to the suspension, which had been conducted by both the FBI and House Un-American Activities Committee, didn't turn up any evidence of communist spies but did indicate that security measures at the fort were lax. The ever-dramatic McCarthy rushed back from his honeymoon to zealously pursue the case, contending that the army was underplaying what he described as an extremely dangerous spy ring working out of the New Jersey military base.

Claims and counterclaims exchanged between McCarthy and army officials growing out of the Fort Monmouth incident led to the senator holding hearings on alleged subversion and espionage within the Army Signal Corps before his Senate Permanent Subcommittee on Investigations from October through December 1953. While the army denied that any documents were missing from Fort Monmouth, McCarthy alleged otherwise, based on assertions from his hearings, which he periodically leaked to a voracious press corps. One witness testified that it was common practice for scientists at Fort Monmouth to take secret material home for after-hours review. Another said that some twenty-six documents were stolen and ferried to East Germany, where government officials were amazed by and scornful of U.S. incompetence and its inability to safeguard top-secret information.

McCarthy's leaks paid off in blaring front-page headlines that generated intense public interest in his cause. "M'Carthy Bares Security Leak to Reich Reds" screamed one top-of-the-page newspaper headline from October 14, 1953. According to the story, McCarthy revealed that a top scientist for the Army Signal Corps had admitted taking forty-three secret documents from Fort Monmouth to his home for "study." After a week of speculation and mounting controversy over the disturbing information gleaned from McCarthy's hearings, the *New York Times* voiced the public's concern, asking, "When will the full story of Fort Monmouth be revealed?"

McCarthy gleefully capitalized on the mounting public hysteria, expanding his probe to Camp Evans, once the site of Guglielmo Marconi's transatlantic radio station and a base under the control of Fort Monmouth. The U.S. Army had created a top-secret research facility at the site, nestled in the farmland of rural Wall Township overlooking the Shark River inlet. Radar had been partly designed and vastly improved at Evans, helping to ensure Allied victory in World War II. After the war, army officials retained the camp as a research facility, relocating and employing German scientists and engineers at the site.

Camp Evans became a prominent target of the ongoing investigation. Some of the most prominent witnesses called to testify at the subcommittee hearings in Washington—Aaron Coleman, Carl Greenblum and Joseph Levitsky—were former researchers at the Evans laboratory. Coleman, a radar officer, had been caught outside the lab with classified information in 1946, while both Greenblum and Levitsky had once carpooled with Julius Rosenberg.

In a highly publicized visit to Camp Evans on October 20, 1953, McCarthy and his entourage, including Roy Cohn, special counsel for the subcommittee, toured the Evans facility. The visit began on a sour note when Cohn was not admitted to the camp because he lacked a proper security clearance. Cohn was agitated by the snub and vowed before witnesses that he

U.S. senator Eugene McCarthy confers with members of his staff (*left to right*, Roy Cohn, Frank Caar, James Juliana and Senator McCarthy) at Camp Evans in Wall Township, a substation of Fort Monmouth involved in radar research, regarding a report that there was a connection between the staff there and Soviet agents in Europe. No such connection was ever proven. *InfoAge Museum.*

Senator McCarthy left Camp Evans with the secretary of the army and the commander of the U.S. Signal Corps. *InfoAge Museum.*

would avenge what he considered an insulting exclusion. (Cohn would later become a prominent figure in the army-McCarthy hearings, during which he was accused of pressuring the army to provide preferential treatment for a friend who was an enlisted man.)

Despite the initial difficulties, however, the tour ended in mutual expressions of goodwill and cooperation. McCarthy revealed, with satisfaction, that more than a dozen workers at the laboratory had been suspended and that his investigation would continue.

"I have been very favorably impressed with the aggressive steps taken…to clear up this situation," the senator said. "An extremely bad and dangerous situation has existed here over the years. Some past and present—until

Senator McCarthy, ever a publicity hound, held an impromptu press conference in the old Marconi Hotel telegraph operators' lounge room at Camp Evans. *InfoAge Museum.*

recently present—employees have been very unfaithful. After seeing the Evans laboratories I am impressed with the tremendous damage a spy could do if he had some access to its classified information."

The suspended Camp Evans employees were joined by a roster of suspended Fort Monmouth workers; by November, that number had risen to thirty-three. In addition, employees under suspicion but not suspended were detailed to work at a cluster of World War II barracks dubbed the "leper colony."

In spite of Senator McCarthy's relentless pursuit of evidence of espionage within the Army Signal Corps and at Camp Evans, weeks of hearings produced absolutely no evidence of subversion or espionage, and no one was ever prosecuted. McCarthy's abrasive manner and relentless tirades earned him numerous enemies, however, including Republican president Dwight D. Eisenhower, who once allegedly described him as a "pimple on the path of progress." (That phrase may have been cleaned up a bit.)

The senator's downslide began with the 1954 army-McCarthy hearings, which were centered on charges that McCarthy and Cohn improperly pressured the army to give preferential treatment to a colleague who was then serving as a private. The hearings, which were broadcast on live television, failed to find McCarthy guilty of any wrongdoing but wreaked tremendous havoc on his public reputation. The television broadcast graphically displayed McCarthy's arrogant, bullying demeanor as never before, and former allies, like FBI head J. Edgar Hoover, began to distance themselves, sensing the senator's fall from grace.

Disheartened by his waning power and influence, McCarthy, always a heavy drinker, sank deeper into alcoholism. Three years after the army hearings, he died at age forty-eight, apparently of cirrhosis of the liver. He left behind a notorious legacy of fear and intimidation, whose victims included the workers at Fort Monmouth and Camp Evans, their lives shattered in a relentless Cold War probe that ultimately failed to produce any evidence of criminality.

For more on the career of Senator McCarthy, see Halberstam, The Fifties. *We would like to thank Fred Carl of InfoAge Museum, located at the former Camp Evans, for his invaluable assistance in this essay. To learn more, visit the museum.*

CHAPTER 17

NEW JERSEY'S NIKES

Like silent sentries awaiting the call to battle, Nike antiaircraft missiles were once scattered throughout strategic areas of New Jersey from Franklin Lakes to Woolwich Township, part of a national defense network poised to confront the unthinkable—an air attack from the Soviet Union's long-range bomber, the TU-95, which could fly six thousand miles without refueling.

The missiles were a response to the ominous threats posed by the Cold War and were an integral component of the elaborate defense structure established in strategic locations throughout New Jersey and across the country, including air defense radar sites, bases for interceptor aircraft, antiaircraft gun batteries, surface-to-air missile sites and command and control facilities. The massive military buildup was designed to defend against the Soviet nuclear threat, and the U.S. early warning system and air defense sites were manned on a twenty-four-hour basis, ready to respond at a moment's notice.

The Continental United States, or CONUS, Air Defense System, including the New Jersey sites, was under the overall control of the North American Air Defense Command, or NORAD, manned by a joint operations group from the U.S. and Canadian air forces and headquartered in Cheyenne Mountain at Colorado Springs, Colorado.

The Nike program, named for the mythical Greek goddess of victory, produced the world's first successful, widely deployed guided surface to air antiaircraft missile system. Within the continental United States, the missiles

The Nike Hercules was nuclear capable. The barometric probe on the nose of this missile reveals that it is nuclear-armed. *NGMMNJ.*

were intended to act as a "last ditch" line of air defense, in case the air force's aircraft failed to destroy attacking bombers.

The first successful firing of a Nike missile, the Nike Ajax, was achieved in 1951. The slender, two-stage guided missile was blasted off its launcher by means of a solid fuel rocket booster that accelerated the missile with a power twenty-five times the force of gravity. The Ajax missile reached speeds of more than 1,600 mph, or Mach 2.5, and could reach targets at altitudes of up to seventy thousand feet. Its range was only thirty miles, however, which was too short a distance to make it truly effective, according to the weapon's detractors.

A close up view of the barometric probe. This device was mounted in the nose of the Hercules and designed to measure altitude and prevent the missile from exploding too close to the ground. *Joseph G. Bilby.*

The Ajax was deployed in 1954, but work on a successor was quickly underway, with the goal of producing a missile with improved speed, range and altitude capabilities, armed with a powerful nuclear warhead. The end result was the Nike Hercules.

With its nuclear capability, a single Nike Hercules missile could obliterate an entire closely spaced formation of attacking aircraft. In addition, it was able to destroy or disable the nuclear weapons aboard any surviving enemy plane, ensuring that they would be unable to detonate even if successfully dropped.

Over their service lives, both Nike missiles were an essential component of a comprehensive air defense system charged with absorbing enough of the weight of an initial attack to avoid governmental paralysis and allow the United States to retaliate with nuclear warfare against the enemy's homeland. The consequences of failure were chilling; if even one bomber penetrated the shield, it could destroy an entire city.

In response to such a disturbing possibility, numerous Nike missile sites were built in defensive rings of steel surrounding major American urban and industrial areas. In New Jersey, the sites were divided into two distinct

National Guard air defense artillerymen were assigned to man several New Jersey Nike bases, like this one, armed with Nike Hercules nuclear capable antiaircraft missiles. *NGMMNJ.*

groups. Locations in the northern part of the state were associated with the former New York Defense Area. The installations were established in Leonardo/Belford/Middletown, Holmdel/Hazlet, Sandy Hook/Fort Hancock, Old Bridge, South Plainfield, Summit/Watchung, Livingston/East Hanover, Wayne/Mountain View, Ramsey/Franklin Lakes and Darlington/Mahwah.

Sites in southern New Jersey were part of the former Philadelphia Defense Area and included Lumberton, Marlton, Erial, Mantua Township and Woolwich Township. North and south, these sites were manned by both regular army and New Jersey National Guard personnel.

A typical Nike air defense position consisted of two separate tracts of land. The Integral Fire Control (IFC) area contained the system's ground-based radar and computer systems designed to protect the site, track hostile aircraft and guide the missiles to their targets. The other tract, known as the Launcher Control Area (LCA), was where the missiles were stored within heavily constructed underground magazines. A massive elevator carried the Nikes to

Part of the "old school" electronics and radar system used in the Nike command and control vans at Sandy Hook. *Joseph G. Bilby.*

the surface of the site, where they were manually pushed by crewmen across two steel rails to one of four launchers. The missiles were mounted on the launchers and then raised to a near-vertical position for firing.

The Nike sites, initially primarily manned by members of the regular army, were, on a growing basis following 1959, staffed by members of the New Jersey Army National Guard, who had previously been responsible for the ninety-millimeter antiaircraft guns that had supplemented the Nikes but were being phased out. A decade later, an estimated four thousand Army Guardsmen were on duty across the country to help protect the United States from a surprise enemy bomber attack, according to an August 1970 article in the *National Guardsman* magazine.

Although the Nike sites were never called into action to meet an external threat, a devastating disaster at the Middletown, New Jersey installation in 1958 ended the lives of ten men. Known at the time as "the world's worst missile disaster," the tragedy occurred on May 22, when eight Nike missiles exploded, killing six regular army soldiers and four civilian technicians.

New Jersey National Guardsmen fueling a Nike Ajax. The fuel was so toxic that protective suits were required for the task. *NGMMNJ.*

Henry Lutz, a twenty-four-year-old independent contractor, was dumping a load of dirt at the site when he was thrown from his truck by a blast from behind. "There was fire all around," Lutz recalled in a newspaper interview thirty years later. "I remember running, running to the fence. Then there was a second explosion behind me that pushed me forward."

Lutz was able to climb over the fence, followed by others who were running for safety. "I couldn't hear anything out of my left ear," he said. "All the whistles, sirens and alarm bells were going off around me." Ernie Giudici, a soldier stationed at the base who lost a friend in the explosion, recalled, "Some of the debris went a mile or so into a farmer's field."

Reports said the explosions rocked the area within a three-mile radius of the launch site, breaking windows and blowing doors open. Frank F. Blaisdell, mayor of Middletown, was at work in his Red Bank lumberyard when he heard the deafening explosions. Blaisdell called the Middletown police chief and asked for a police escort to the site. Upon arriving, he was confronted by a scene of unspeakable destruction and carnage.

"It was a terrible sight," he said. "The men were gone."

Within hours of the explosion, journalists from around the world were swarming the area. Brigadier General Charles B. Duff, commander of the army's New York defense area, described the accident as a disaster that "couldn't happen, but did."

The subsequent investigation revealed that the explosion occurred while army personnel were installing safety and arming mechanisms on the missiles, although the exact cause has never been discovered. Two of the three warheads on one of the missiles had been removed to gain access, when the third one suddenly detonated. In addition to destroying the other six aboveground missiles in the vicinity, a flying red-hot pellet apparently ignited the booster of the nearest missile in an adjoining section, blasting it into the side of a nearby hill. Fortunately, the Ajax warhead failed to detonate.

As part of the detailed investigation that ensued, army officials attended a town meeting called by the mayor of Middletown to assuage public concerns about the disaster. Army lawyers arrived to settle claims from local residents, ranging from damaged fire hoses to broken windows, that would total an estimated $12,000.

Beyond repair, however, was the public's perception of the army's air defense program. In the wake of the disaster, newspaper and magazine editors mocked army claims that a Nike installation was no more dangerous than a gas station.

Today, the only evidence of the horrific accident is a memorial to the men who died, which stands at Fort Hancock, a former military installation at Sandy Hook that is now a national park. The monument, which is in the form of two rockets symbolizing the Nike Ajax and Nike Hercules missiles, overlooks Sandy Hook Bay. Sandy Hook was the site of another Nike base, one of the few that remain intact. It is now open for guided tours.

The Nike program wasn't the only New Jersey–related air defense effort that witnessed a tragic accident during the Cold War era. In January 1961,

Opposite, top: Members of the Fort Hancock Nike Site Volunteers Association, veterans of the Nike Air Defense organization, at the command and control center on Sandy Hook. The organization provides tours of the site for visitors. *Left to right*: Paul Klco, Jim Langandoen, Bill Jackson, Bob Bohalander and Pete DeMarco. *Joseph G. Bilby.*

Opposite, bottom: A "Texas tower" identical to the one that toppled off the New Jersey coast in January 1961, under construction. *Joseph G. Bilby.*

twenty-eight men were killed after the collapse of Texas Tower #4, a massive radar installation in the Atlantic Ocean, some seventy-five miles off the New Jersey coast.

The tower, one of three similar installations off the East Coast named "Texas Towers" for their resemblance to offshore Gulf of Mexico oil rigs, was designed to provide early warning in case of an enemy air attack so that Nike missiles could respond. Dubbed "Old Shaky" by the men who worked aboard it because of its tendency to shift in the ever-moving ocean, the structure was built on three pilings in 185 feet of water.

Two previous hurricanes had damaged the tower's underwater bracings, so the structure was particularly vulnerable when a vicious winter storm struck, battering the tower with forty-mile-per-hour winds and thirty-foot-high waves. A navy supply ship received an ominous message from the tower's personnel on Sunday afternoon: "Things getting worse, tower shaking and beginning to get loose."

Evacuation plans were formed to rescue the crew by helicopter during a lull in the storm, but at 7:30 p.m., the tower fell, plunging the men into the frigid Atlantic waters. Following an intensive air and sea search, the twenty-eight men—fourteen air force personnel and fourteen civilians—were presumed dead.

The horrific disaster led to a reassessment of the towers' effectiveness, and the other two off the Massachusetts coast were closed shortly thereafter.

The Nike program itself, however, continued for more than a decade. In its 1970 article, the *National Guardsman* detailed the story of the "missile-

The aircraft carrier USS *Wasp* engaging in a fruitless search for survivors of the Texas tower disaster. *Joseph G. Bilby.*

minding Minute Men," the army Guardsmen working at the Nike sites whose "everyday job is to help protect the United States from surprise enemy bomber attack."

"Professionalism and personnel stability are key elements in the success of the Army National Guard's on-site NIKE-HERCULES program," the article noted. "These on-site missile units are today's embodiment of a concept of fixed defense that goes back to Colonial days, when Militiamen manned seacoast artillery against the threat of seaborne invasion or pirates." Interestingly, testing proved that the National Guardsmen were indeed more effective than their regular army counterparts, which veterans of the program attribute to the greater personnel stability of the state-based units.

Despite the program's apparent effectiveness, however, in 1970, there were looming concerns about its future. "More recently, several Active Army and National Guard missile sites have been cut from the program, primarily a result of succeeding budget squeezes," the article noted. "Speculation on further reduction in the air defense program at this point would be pure guesswork."

Indeed, the glory days of the Nike sites were on the wane due to a number of factors, including new threats posed by intercontinental ballistic missiles as opposed to long-range strategic bombers, the expense associated with the Vietnam War, a general desire to trim budgets and changing national and military priorities. In 1974, the last remaining sites were closed.

Thanks to a group of New Jersey Air Defense Artillery veterans, the history of the state's Nike bases endures. Tours of the Sandy Hook installation, given by extremely knowledgeable veteran tour guides, are available to the public.

For more information, see http://ny56nike.weebly.com/.

For an example of a Nike Hercules crew in action, see http://www.youtube.com/watch?v=j_qb_Aruq2s.

The authors would like to thank Ernie Giudici, James Cory Newman, Bob Preston, Bill Jackson, Paul Klco and all the members of the Fort Hancock Nike Site NY-56 Volunteers Association for their invaluable assistance in this story. For more, be sure to visit Sandy Hook and take the tour.

NEW JERSEY HISTORIC MILITARY SITES AND MUSEUMS WORTH VISITING

Fort Hancock

The Sandy Hook peninsula, with the Atlantic Ocean on one side and Raritan Bay on the other, is rich with New Jersey history, dating from the time it was first rounded by Verrazano in 1524. The lighthouse at Sandy Hook, erected in 1764, on what is the gateway to New York Harbor, is the oldest existing lighthouse in the United States. Loyalists established a fortified camp and raider base around the lighthouse during the Revolution, and New Jersey militiamen and federal Sea Fencibles garrisoned forts on Sandy Hook during the War of 1812. A coast defense fort was partially constructed on Sandy Hook in the late 1850s but was abandoned when the Civil War proved such forts vulnerable to artillery.

Sandy Hook served as the U.S. Army Ordnance Corps' first weapons and ammunition proving ground from 1874 to 1919, and Fort Hancock, named for Civil War major general Winfield Scott Hancock, was constructed in the 1890s. Fort Hancock's guns were fully manned during World Wars I and II and after the war, as continental defense weaponry evolved from coastal guns to antiaircraft artillery to Nike antiaircraft missiles. It was the site of a prison for military offenders during the latter part of World War II. The fort was decommissioned in 1974 and subsequently became part of the Gateway National Recreation Area. Much of the fort remains, and there is also a museum dedicated to its history on the site.

Sandy Hook is also the site of a Nike antiaircraft missile base that was, along with a number of other such bases in New Jersey and elsewhere, part of America's Cold War defense system. The base is open for tours.

Location and Contact: 128 South Hartshorne Drive, Highlands, New Jersey 07732. (718) 354-4606

Hours: 5:00 a.m. to 8:00 p.m. This includes times the beach is open to fishermen. For hours of access and ranger or volunteer tours at the lighthouse, fortifications and Nike base, see http://www.nps.gov/gate/planyourvisit/sandy-hook-hours.htm. For information on Nike tours specifically, see http://ny56nike.weebly.com/.

Admission: Free

http://www.nps.gov/gate/historyculture/hancock.htm

http://www.facebook.com/GatewayNPS?sk=wall

FORT MOTT STATE PARK

Fort Mott was envisioned as part of a three-fort defense system designed for the defense of the Delaware River against enemy ships in the post–Civil War era and was originally planned to have eleven gun emplacements housing twenty heavy artillery pieces and a mortar battery with six massive mortars. The current fortifications were completed in 1896. The installation was named for Gershom Mott, a New Jersey native who served as an officer in the Mexican and Civil Wars and commanded the state's National Guard in the postwar period.

Regular army soldiers were stationed at Fort Mott from 1897 to 1922, and the federal government maintained a caretaker detachment at the fort between 1922 and 1943, during which time the fort's guns were dismantled. The fort was declared "surplus property" in 1943. New Jersey acquired the military reservation as a historic site and state park in 1947, and it was opened to the public on June 24, 1951.

Although Fort Mott was disarmed long ago and the guns are gone, emplacements and magazines still line an impressive 750-foot-long, 35-foot-thick poured concrete parapet, which is buttressed by an additional 30 feet of sand and earth. The site, maintained by the New Jersey Department of Environmental Protection, provides a self-guided tour with interpretive signs. There are eleven stops on the tour, and the visitor center features exhibits on the fort's history. It is also the southern anchor for the New Jersey Coastal Heritage Trail.

Location and Contact: 454 Fort Mott Road, Pennsville, New Jersey 08070. (856) 935-3218.
Hours: Daily from 8:00 a.m. to 7:30 p.m.
Admission: Free
Guided tours available for school and other groups. Call for information on special events and programs.
http://www.state.nj.us/dep/parksandforests/parks/fortmott.htm
http://www.facebook.com/pages/Fort-Mott-State-Park/529926737026299?fref=ts.

HANCOCK HOUSE

Built in 1734, the Hancock House was the home of a prominent Salem County family and is an excellent example of English Quaker pattern brick houses associated with the lower Delaware Valley and southwestern New Jersey.

Perhaps the most egregious British raid of the Revolution had this house as its focal point. On the night of March 20–21, 1778, Major John Simcoe's Loyalists conducted a surprise attack on the Hancock's Bridge garrison, killing everyone they could find in the vicinity, including men they encountered along the road; twenty to thirty militiamen sleeping in the Hancock house; and the house's owner, Judge William Hancock, and his brother, who happened to be noted local Loyalists. After the war, Simcoe bragged about the massacre of the militiamen as a stellar surprise operation but expressed sorrow at the "unfortunate circumstances" of the bayoneting of the judge and his brother, stating that "events like these are the real miseries of war."

Cornelia Hancock, the saintly New Jersey Civil War nurse known as "America's Florence Nightingale," was the great-granddaughter of William Hancock.

Location and Contact: 3 Front Street, Hancock's Bridge, New Jersey 08038 (856) 935-4373, Fax: (856) 935-2079.
Hours: Wednesdays through Saturdays, 10:00 a.m. to 12:00 p.m., and 1:00 p.m. to 4:00 p.m. Sundays: 1:00 p.m. to 4:00 p.m. Closed Mondays and Tuesdays, most state and federal holidays and Wednesdays following Monday or Tuesday holidays.
Admission: Free
Group tours and school programs available by reservation.

http://www.state.nj.us/dep/parksandforests/historic/hancockhouse/
hancockhouse-index.htm
http://www.facebook.com/pages/Hancock-
House/111902012158201?fref=ts

HISTORIC NEW BRIDGE LANDING PARK

New Bridge, in Bergen County, was a strategic Hackensack River crossing throughout the American Revolution. Its homes served as headquarters for commanders of both sides, and both armies camped on its hills and fields. Skirmishes between Loyalists and Patriots were a commonplace feature at New Bridge throughout the conflict. Soldiers passed this gateway to New Jersey's hinterland so often that the still-standing "Steuben House," confiscated by the state from a Loyalist and owned by Baron von Steuben for a time after the war, is said to have seen more of the Revolution pass by than any other house in America.

American troops fleeing the victorious British from Fort Lee crossed the Hackensack at New Bridge, Thomas Paine reportedly penned the first draft of *The American Crisis* there, and most of the military notables of the Revolution, from George Washington on down, made a stop, at one time or another, at the little mill town.

The site has been preserved and restored by adjoining towns, Bergen County and the Bergen County Historical Society and hosts Revolutionary War living history encampments a number of times a year, as well as other events.

Location and Contact: 1201 Main Street, River Edge, New Jersey, 07661. commission@newbridgelanding.org

Hours: Sunrise to sunset, with historic houses open during most events. For a walking tour app, see http://www.bergencountyhistory.org/mobile/hnbl_tour.html#PageHome.

Admission: Free. Donations to the Bergen County Historical Association preservation fund are welcome.

http://www.bergencountyhistory.org/Pages/events.html

INFOAGE

Located in Wall Township on the site of Camp Evans, a former adjunct facility to Fort Monmouth, the InfoAge museum is dedicated to creating an "Information Age Learning Center" in historic buildings that once housed the staff of the Marconi transatlantic wireless transmittal station. The site was also a World War I overseas communications station and a major World War II and Cold War–era radar laboratory as a part of the larger Fort Monmouth complex. It was the site of a famous visit by Senator Joseph McCarthy during his investigation of alleged Communist infiltration of the Fort Monmouth Signal Corps installation. Exhibits display the evolution of military radio and radar technology over those years.

Camp Evans is listed on the National Register of Historic Sites, and the National Park Service has approved an application to use thirty-seven acres of the camp and all the buildings in the historic district to help improve the public understanding of science, technology and science history, honouring the communication pioneers of wireless, World War I, World War II, space exploration and the Cold War.

Location and Contact: 2201 Marconi Road, Wall Township, New Jersey, 07719. (732) 280-3000.

Hours: 1:00 p.m. to 5:00 p.m., Wednesday, Saturday and Sunday.

Admission: A suggested five-dollar donation per person.

http://www.infoage.org/

http://www.campevans.org/

MILLVILLE ARMY AIRFIELD MUSEUM

The Millville Airport was dedicated as "America's First Defense Airport" on August 2, 1941, by local, state and federal officials. In less than a year, construction began, and in January 1943, the Millville Army Air Field opened as a gunnery school for fighter pilots. Training began with Curtiss P-40F Warhawks, but after a few weeks, the P-40s were replaced by Republic P-47 Thunderbolts. About 1,500 pilots received advanced fighter training in the Thunderbolt at Millville before it closed in 1946.

Following the war, the airfield was declared excess federal property and returned to the city of Millville. Most of the buildings were converted to apartments for veterans' housing. The apartments were phased out by the early 1970s, and the airport soon became a southern New Jersey industrial and aviation hub.

The museum originated with the collection of Michal T. Stowe, who, as a teenager in the 1970s, began exploring abandoned World War II bunkers and collecting artifacts and documents relating to the airport. In 1983, Stowe approached the city to request a permanent location at the airport to display his collection, which remains the cornerstone of the Millville Army Air Field Museum.

The collection has grown through donations of time, effort and artifacts from the local community and veterans who served at Millville, and the museum has gained recognition for its contributions to World War II aviation history.

Location and Contact: 1 Ledden Street, Millville Airport, Millville, New Jersey 08332. (856) 327-2347

Hours: 10:00 a.m. to 4:00 p.m. Tuesday through Sunday. Monday visits may be scheduled by appointment. For group tours, call (856) 327-2347.
http://www.p47millville.org/museum/
http://www.facebook.com/pages/Millville-Army-Air-Field-Museum/149862535026130?fref=ts

MONMOUTH BATTLEFIELD STATE PARK

The longest single-day battle of the American Revolution took place in the fields and forests that now make up Monmouth Battlefield State Park on June 28, 1778. Although the configuration of the landscape has been somewhat modified by nineteenth-century farming practices, the park preserves a splendid pre-industrial rural landscape of hilly farmland and hedgerows. There are miles of hiking and horseback riding trails, picnic areas and a restored Revolutionary War farmhouse. Well-marked trails with accompanying brochures enable the visitor to accurately follow the course of the battle across the field. A new visitor center dedicated on June 14, 2013, houses exhibits that deal with the battle, as well as the use of part of the parkland as a Civil War rendezvous camp that processed and organized over three thousand soldiers in the Fourteenth, Twenty-eighth, Twenty-ninth and part of the Thirty-fifth New Jersey Infantry Regiments in 1862 and 1863.

The annual Battle of Monmouth reenactment hosted by the park is a significant event that draws a large number of Revolutionary War reenactors and visiting spectators.

Location and Contact: 16 Business Route 33, Manalapan, New Jersey 07726. (732) 462-9616
Park hours: Daily: 8:00 p.m. to 4:30 p.m.
Visitor Center Hours: 9:00 a.m. to 4:00 p.m.
Admission: Free.
A variety of interpretive and educational programs are available.
http://www.state.nj.us/dep/parksandforests/parks/monbat.html
http://hwcdn.net/a5h8p3i4/cds/dep/monbattle_09.mp4
http://www.facebook.com/pages/Monmouth-Battlefield-State-Park/104089286293269?fref=ts

MORRISTOWN NATIONAL HISTORICAL PARK

Morristown National Historical Park, established in 1933, is the oldest National Historic Park in the country. The park's mission is to commemorate the encampment of General George Washington's Continental army at Morristown over the winter of 1779–80, the worst winter of the eighteenth century. Morristown was a strong Patriot town and a perfect location for a base with the British occupying New York, and the Americans had spent the remainder of the winter there after their victories at Trenton and Princeton in 1776 and early 1777. Washington's outposts could observe British movements and were protected from surprise by the Watchung Mountains.

Features of the park include the Ford Mansion, used by Washington for his headquarters in 1779–80 and reconstructed soldier huts at Jockey Hollow, as well as a research library and archive and a museum with an extensive display of equipment, artifacts and art connected with the era.
Location: http://www.nps.gov/morr/planyourvisit/directions.htm
Hours: Vary by season: http://www.nps.gov/morr/planyourvisit/hours.htm
Admission: Ford Mansion, adults, four dollars; children, free. Jockey Hollow and the Wick house, free to all.
http://www.nps.gov/morr/index.htm
http://www.facebook.com/pages/Morristown-National-Historical-Park/146510708712035?fref=ts

NATIONAL GUARD MILITIA MUSEUM OF NEW JERSEY AT SEA GIRT

The mission of the National Guard Militia Museum of New Jersey is to preserve and explain the military heritage of New Jersey and enhance public understanding of how armed conflicts and military institutions have shaped our state and national experience. The museum collects, preserves and displays artifacts, documents and memorabilia that have specific historical significance to the Army National Guard, the Air National Guard and the Naval Militia of New Jersey.

The museum presents the role of the New Jersey Militia and National Guard within the context of the larger history of the state, using original and reproduction uniforms, weapons, photographs, artifacts and art from the period of Dutch, Swedish and British colonization through the War for Independence, Civil War and World Wars I and II to the present day, paying particular attention to the diversity of the New Jersey citizen soldier and his or her experience.

The National Guard Militia Museum of New Jersey is also the home of the Center for U.S. War Veterans' Oral History Project. It is the center's mission to collect and preserve the memories of veterans through recorded oral history interviews, and it does so in cooperation with the Library of Congress.

Location and Contact: National Guard Training Center, Sea Girt Avenue & Camp Drive, Sea Girt, New Jersey 08750. (732) 974-5966

Hours: Open seven days a week year round from 10:00 a.m. to 3:00 p.m. Closed on state holidays.

Admission: free

School and group tours available.

http://www.nj.gov/military/museum/index.html

http://www.facebook.com/pages/National-Guard-Militia-Museum-of-New-Jersey/127004387321616?fref=ts

NAVAL AIR STATION WILDWOOD AVIATION MUSEUM

Naval Air Station (NAS) Wildwood Aviation Museum is a nonprofit museum located at the Cape May Airport inside historic Hangar #1. Commissioned in April 1943, the original naval air station served as an active dive-bomber squadron training facility during World War II. Today, Hangar #1 has been restored and transformed into an aviation museum that houses a number of aircraft, engines, special exhibits and educational interactive displays. The "Avenger" torpedo bomber on display was manufactured at the General Motors Eastern Aircraft Division in Ewing Township, outside Trenton, in 1943. The Ewing factory turned out 7,546 Avengers during the war. The museum invites visitors to explore aviation, New Jersey, military and World War II history through "hands-on," fun and educational activities for the entire family in a ninety-two-thousand-square-foot sampling of New Jersey's war effort in the 1940s. Photography is encouraged.

Location and Contact: 500 Forrestal Road, Cape May Airport, New Jersey 08242. (609) 886-8787. aviationmuseum@comcast.net 501(c)(3) nonprofit corporation. Contributions are tax-deductible to the extent allowed by law.

Hours: April 1 through October 12: Open daily 9:00 a.m. to 5:00 p.m.; October 13 through November 30: Open daily 9:00 a.m. to 4:00 p.m.; December 1 through March 31: Monday–Friday, 9:00 a.m. to 4:00 p.m., Saturday–Sunday, closed.

Holiday Hours: Christmas Eve: 9:00 a.m. to 1:00 p.m.; Christmas Day: closed; New Year's Eve; 9:00 a.m. to 1:00 p.m.; New Year's Day: closed.

Admission: Adults: ten dollars; seniors: ten dollars; children, three through twelve: eight dollars; children under three: free.

http://usnasw.org/

http://www.facebook.com/aviationmuseum

NEW JERSEY STATE MUSEUM CIVIL WAR FLAGS ANNEX

A joint project of the New Jersey Civil War Heritage Association and the New Jersey State Museum, with the assistance of the Sons of Union Veterans of the Civil War, the annex displays five historic New Jersey Civil War flags from the museum's vast collection. Every six months, the flags, displayed in acid-free exhibit cases, are rotated. The rotation event features an educational gallery walk by a New Jersey Civil War scholar. In addition to flags, the exhibit is enhanced by an illustrated narrative on the role of New Jersey and its citizens in the Civil War, as well as a rotating display featuring firearms, equipment, photographs and military documents from the New Jersey State Archives collections and on loan from private collectors. New artifacts and archival materials will be exhibited periodically through the end of the Civil War Sesquicentennial in 2015.

Location: New Jersey Department of State building galleries, 225 West State Street, Trenton, New Jersey 08625 (corner of Calhoun and West State Streets).

Hours: Open to the public Monday through Friday, 9:00 a.m. to 5:00 p.m. Closed on state holidays.

Admission: free.

http://www.nj.gov/state/museum/dos_museum_exhibit_civil-war-flags.html
For more on New Jersey's Civil War role, see http://www.njcivilwar.org/ and http://www.facebook.com/NJCivilWar?fref=ts

New Jersey Vietnam Veterans Memorial

The New Jersey Vietnam Veterans Memorial, located in Holmdel on the grounds of the PNC Bank Arts Center located at Garden State Parkway exit 116, is intended to honor New Jerseyans who served in the Vietnam War, especially the 1,561 men and 1 woman from the state who lost their lives in the conflict. The design was created by Hien Nguyen in 1988, and the completed memorial was officially dedicated on May 7, 1995. The memorial is open twenty-four hours a day every day of the year, and admission is free. Guided tours by docent volunteer New Jersey veterans are available for groups.

The memorial is a circular pavilion, containing 366 eight-foot-tall black granite panels, each one representing a day of the year, and casualties are listed by the day on which they lost their lives. The center of the pavilion features a red oak, the New Jersey state tree, and three statues: a dying soldier, a nurse tending to his wounds and another soldier standing by their side, representing those who died, the women who served and those who returned. The Vietnam Era Museum and Educational Center, which explains the war and the era and their effect on the state and country, provides a lens into history for the visitor.

Location and Contact: New Jersey Vietnam Veterans' Memorial Foundation, #1 Memorial Lane, PO Box 648, Holmdel, New Jersey, 07733. (732) 335-0033

Hours: Museum is open Tuesday through Saturday and selected holidays, 10:00 a.m. to 4:00 p.m.

Admission: Adults, seven dollars; senior citizens and students, five dollars; children ten years of age or younger, free; veterans and active duty military personnel, free.

Guided and group tours are available.
http://www.njvvmf.org/
http://www.facebook.com/NJVVMF

TRENTON OLD BARRACKS

The Trenton Old Barracks Museum, built in 1758, is the only French and Indian War–era barracks still standing. It was also used during the Revolutionary War by both the Hessian occupiers of Trenton in 1776 and American forces thereafter. In the years after the Revolution, it was used as housing, and the central part of the building was torn down to allow a street to pass through. Purchased by the DAR and presented to the state in the early twentieth century, the Old Barracks was eventually restored to its original configuration and serves as a museum commemorating the role of New Jersey in both the Colonial Wars and the Revolution.

The site hosts a number of events during the year, including summer day camps for students, living history encampments and permanent and changing exhibits on the era.

Location and Contact: 101 Barrack Street, Trenton, New Jersey 08608. (609) 396-1776

Hours: Monday to Saturday, 10:00 a.m. to 5:00 p.m. Closed Thanksgiving, December 24–25, January 1 and Easter.

Admission: Adults, eight dollars; seniors (sixty-two and over) and students (age six and above) with ID, six dollars; children under five with families and Association Members, free.

School and other tours available.
http://www.barracks.org/
https://www.facebook.com/pages/The-Old-Barracks/110676295637353?ref=ts

THE USS *NEW JERSEY*

The battleship USS *New Jersey* was built at the Philadelphia Naval Shipyard and launched on December 7, 1942—just a year after the Pearl Harbor Attack brought America into World War II. It was commissioned on May

23, 1943, and served in World War II in the Pacific Theater. The ship was decommissioned on June 30, 1948, and then recommissioned on November 21, 1950, for service in Korea. Decommissioned on August 21, 1957, the *New Jersey* was recommissioned again, after modernizing work at the Philadelphia Shipyard, on April 6, 1968, for service in Vietnam. It was decommissioned yet again on December 17, 1969, but returned to service on December 28, 1982, at Long Beach, California. The ship was decommissioned for the final time on February 8, 1991, and returned to the Philadelphia shipyard on November 11, 1999, for restoration and service as a museum. The *New Jersey* crossed the Delaware to Camden in October 2001, where it has been serving as a museum and memorial ever since.

Location and contact: 100 Clinton Street, Camden, New Jersey. For tickets, call (866) 877-6262, ext. 108.

Hours: Variable according to season. For complete information, see the website: http://www.battleshipnewjersey.org/.

BIBLIOGRAPHY

BOOKS

Adelberg, Michael S. *The American Revolution in Monmouth County: The Theatre of Spoil and Destruction*. Charleston, SC: The History Press, 2010.

Bauer, K. Jack. *The Mexican War, 1846–1848*. New York: MacMillan, 1974.

Berhow, Mark. *U.S. Strategic and Defensive Missile Systems: 1950–2004*. Oxford, UK: Osprey Publishing, 2005.

Bilby, Joseph G., and Katherine Bilby Jenkins. *Monmouth Court House: The Battle That Made the American Army*. Yardley, PA: Westholme Publishing, 2010.

Bilby, Joseph G., ed. *New Jersey Goes to War: Biographies of 150 New Jerseyans Caught Up in the Struggle of the Civil War, including Soldiers, Civilians, Men, Women, Heroes, Scoudrels—and a Heroic Horse*. Hightstown, NJ: Longstreet House, 2010.

Bilby, Joseph G., James M. Madden and Harry Ziegler. *Hidden History of New Jersey*. Charleston, SC: The History Press, 2011.

———. *350 Years of New Jersey History; From Stuyvesant to Sandy*. Charleston, SC: The History Press, 2013.

Bill, Alfred Hoyt. *New Jersey and the Revolutionary War*. Princeton, NJ: D. Van Nostrand, 1964.

Buchholz, Margaret Thomas. *Shore Chronicles: Diaries and Travelers' Tales from the Jersey Shore, 1764–1955*. Harvey Cedars, NJ: Down the Shore Publishing, 1999.

Coakley, Leo J. *Jersey Troopers: A Fifty-Year History of the New Jersey State Police*. New Brunswick, NJ: Rutgers Press, 1971.

Cooper, Jerry. *The Rise of the National Guard: The Evolution of the American Militia, 1865–1920*. Lincoln: University of Nebraska Press, 1997.

Cunningham, John T. *The Uncertain Revolution: Washington and the Continental Army at Morristown*. West Creek, NJ: Down the Shore Publishing, 2007.

Cutchins, John A. *History of the Twenty-Ninth Division, "Blue and Gray," 1917– 1919*. Philadelphia: 29th Division Committee, 1919.

Di Ionno, Mark. *A Guide to New Jersey's Revolutionary War Trail for Families and History Buffs*. New Brunswick, NJ: Rutgers Press, 2000.

Essex Troop. *History of the Essex Troop, 1890–1925*. Newark: Essex Troop, 1926.

Fabend, Firth Haring. *New Netherland in a Nutshell: A Concise History of the Dutch Colony in North America*. Albany, NY: New Netherland Institute, 2012.

Faulk, Odie B., and Joseph A. Stout Jr. *The Mexican War: Changing Interpretations*. Chicago: Swallow Press, 1973.

Fleming, Thomas. *New Jersey: A History*. New York: W.W. Norton, 1977.

Foster, James Y. *New Jersey and the Rebellion: A History of the Services of the Troops and People of New Jersey in Aid of the Union Cause*. Newark: Dennis & Company, 1874.

Gabrielan, Randall. *Explosion at Morgan: The World War I Middlesex Munitions Disaster*. Charleston, SC: The History Press, 2012.

————. *Hoboken: History & Architecture at a Glance.* Atglen, PA: Schiffer Publishing, 2010.

Gannon, Michael. *Operation Drumbeat: The Dramatic True Story of Germany's First U-Boat Attacks along the American Coast in World War II.* New York: Harper & Rowe, 1990.

Gentile, Gary. *Shipwrecks of New Jersey.* Norwalk CT: Sea Sports, 1988.

Gillette, William. *Jersey Blue: Civil War Politics in New Jersey—1854–1865.* New Brunswick, NJ: Rutgers, 1995.

Green, Howard L. *Words That Make New Jersey History: A Primary Source Reader.* Expanded edition. New Brunswick, NJ: Rivergate Books, 2009.

Guernsey, R.S. *New York City and Vicinity During the War of 1812, Being a Military, Civic and Financial Local History of that Period.* New York: Charles L. Woodward, 1889.

Halberstam, David. *The Fifties.* New York: Villard Press, 1953.

Hans, Jim. *100 Hoboken Firsts.* Hoboken, NJ: Hoboken Historical Museum, 2005.

Hickey, Donald R. *The War of 1812: A Forgotten Conflict* Chicago: University of Illinois Press, 1989.

Jacobs, Jaap. *The Colony of New Netherland: A Dutch Settlement in Seventeenth Century America,* Ithaca, NY: Cornell University Press, 2009.

Johnson, Ray Neil. *Heaven, Hell or Hoboken.* Cleveland, OH: O.S. Hubbell Printing, 1919.

Kennett, Lee. *GI: The American Soldier in World War II.* New York: Charles Scribner's Sons, 1987.

Kull, Irving S. *New Jersey: A History.* 4 vols. New York: American Historical Society, 1930.

Kurzman, Dan. *No Greater Glory: The Four Immortal Chaplains and the Sinking of the Dorchester in World War II.* New York: Random House, 2004.

Lee, Francis Bazley, ed. *New Jersey as a Colony and State.* 4 vols. New York: Publishing Society of New Jersey, 1903.

Lender, Mark Edward. *One State in Arms: A Short Military History of New Jersey.* Trenton: New Jersey Historical Commission, 1991.

Lockard, Duane. *The New Jersey Governor: A Study in Political Power.* New York: Van Nostrand, 1964.

Lundin, Leonard. *Cockpit of the Revolution: The War for Independence in New Jersey.* Princeton, NJ: Princeton University Press, 1940.

Lurie, Maxine N., and Marc Mappen, eds. *Encyclopedia of New Jersey.* New Brunswick, NJ: Rutgers Press, 2004.

Lurie, Maxine N., and Richard Veit, eds. *New Jersey: A History of the Garden State.* New Brunswick, NJ: Rutgers, 2012.

Mahon, John K. *History of the Militia and National Guard.* New York: MacMillan, 1983.

Maltz, Leora, ed. *The Cold War Period, 1945–1992.* New York: Greenhaven Press, 2003.

Mappen, Marc. *Jerseyana: The Underside of New Jersey History.* New Brunswick, NJ: Rutgers Press, 1992.

———. *There's More to New Jersey Than the Sopranos.* New Brunswick, NJ: Rivergate Books, 2009.

Millman, Chad. *The Detonators: The Secret Plot to Destroy America and an Epic Hunt for Justice.* New York: Little, Brown and Company, 2006.

Mitnick, Barbara, ed. *New Jersey in the American Revolution.* New Brunswick, NJ: Rivergate Books, 2005.

Robinson, Brigadier General (retired) Paul M., and Dr. Abe Bortz. *The United States Army: Protector of Our Liberties & Defender of Proud Heritage.* Alexandria, VA: U.S. Army, 1963.

State of New Jersey. *Adjutant General's Report, Trenton.* Various years, 1848–1929. Trenton: State of New Jersey.

———. *Historical and Pictorial Review of the National Guard of the State of New Jersey.* Baton Rouge, LA: Army and Navy Publishing Company, 1940.

———. *Record of Officers and Enlisted Men of New Jersey in the War with Mexico, 1846–1848.* Trenton: State of New Jersey.

Stellhorn, Paul A., and Michael J. Birkner. *The Governors of New Jersey: 1664–1974.* Trenton: New Jersey Historical Commission, 1982.

Thomas, Lately. *When Even Angels Wept.* New York: William Morrow & Co. Inc., 1973.

Van Winkle, Daniel. *Old Bergen: History and Reminiscences with Maps and Illustrations.* Jersey City: John W. Harrison, 1902.

Volkman, Ernest. *Espionage: The Greatest Spy Operations of the Twentieth Century.* New York: John Wiley & Sons, 1995.

Wilson, Harold F., ed. *Outline History of New Jersey.* New Brunswick, NJ: Rutgers Press, 1950.

Winkler, John F. *Wabash 1791: St. Clair's Defeat.* Oxford, UK: Osprey, 2011.

Witcover, Jules. *Sabotage at Black Tom: Imperial Germany's Secret War in America, 1914–1917.* Chapel Hill, NC: Algonquin Books of Chapel Hill, 1989.

Ziegler-McPherson, Christina. *Immigrants in Hoboken: One-Way Ticket, 1845–1985.* Charleston, SC: The History Press, 2011.

ARTICLES

Blackman, Ann. "Fatal Cruise of the *Princeton*." *Navy History*, September 2005.

Dunn, Captain Samuel J. "Merritt Dispatch," pamphlet produced by Camp Merritt, May 30, 1919.

Harnes, John A. "Middletown Recalls 1958 Nike Missile Explosion." *Asbury Park Press*, May 22, 1988.

Johnson, William N. "Camp Merritt." *Proceedings of the New Jersey Historical Society* 9, New Series, no. 4 (October 1924).

Kearny, Thomas. "Gen. Stephen Watts Kearny." *Proceedings of the New Jersey Historical Society* 11, no. 1 (January 1926).

Love, Kenneth. "Hope for Radar Men Ends; Tapping From Hulk Stops." *New York Times*, January 17, 1961.

Walker, Luther. "The Story of Missile-minding Minutemen." *National Guardsman*, August 1970.

NEWSPAPERS

Asbury Park Press

Bergen (NJ) Record

Cleveland Plain Dealer

Englewood (NJ) Press

Newark (NJ) Evening News

Newark (NJ) Sunday Call

New York Evening Post

BIBLIOGRAPHY

New York Times

Twin Falls (ID) News

MISCELLANEOUS DOCUMENTS

State of New Jersey Adjutant General's Office. "Miscellaneous Organizations
National Guard and State Militia, Outline History." 1923.

ABOUT THE AUTHORS

Joseph G. Bilby was born in Newark, New Jersey. He received his BA and MA degrees in history from Seton Hall University and served as a lieutenant in the First Infantry Division in Vietnam in 1966–67. Mr. Bilby is retired from the New Jersey Department of Labor and is currently part-time assistant curator of the New Jersey National Guard and Militia Museum in Sea Girt, New Jersey; a member of the New Jersey Civil War Sesquicentennial Committee; and a freelance writer, lecturer and historical consultant. He is the author, editor or coauthor of seventeen books and over four hundred articles on New Jersey history, folklore and military history. Mr. Bilby has received the Jane Clayton Award for contributions to Monmouth County history, as well as an award from the New Jersey Historical Commission for his contributions to the state's military history.

James M. Madden was born in Jersey City, New Jersey, and received his BS in marketing from Saint Peter's College. He is a political consultant who has contributed articles to many Civil War publications and projects, including the New Jersey Civil War Sesquicentennial Committee publications *New Jersey Goes to War* and *New Jersey's Civil War Odyssey*, and he is coauthor of *Hidden History of New Jersey*. He is also a trustee and treasurer of the New Jersey Civil War Heritage Association and its 150th Anniversary Committee, treasurer of the Lincoln Group of New York and member of the Association of Professional Genealogists and Hudson County Genealogical & Historical Society.

ABOUT THE AUTHORS

HARRY ZIEGLER was born in Neptune, New Jersey. He received his BA in English from Monmouth University and his MEd from Georgian Court College. He worked for many years at the *Asbury Park Press*, New Jersey's second-largest newspaper, rising from reporter to bureau chief to editor and managing editor of the paper. He is currently associate principal of Bishop George Ahr High School in Edison, New Jersey, and is coauthor of *Asbury Park: A Brief History*, *Hidden History of New Jersey* and *Asbury Park Reborn*.